Junior
Encyclopedia

Miles
KeLLy

First published in 2012 by Miles Kelly Publishing Ltd
Harding's Barn, Bardfield End Green, Thaxted, Essex, CM6 3PX, UK

This edition printed 2014

4 6 8 10 9 7 5 3

Publishing Director Belinda Gallagher
Creative Director Jo Cowan
Managing Editor Amanda Askew
Editorial Assistant Amy Johnson
Cover Designer Simon Lee
Designer Kayleigh Allen
Indexer Marie Lorimer
Production Manager Elizabeth Collins
Reprographics Stephan Davis, Thom Allaway, Jennifer Cozens,
Anthony Cambray
Assets Lorraine King

ISBN 978-1-78209-522-4

Printed in China

British Library Cataloguing-in-Publication Data
A catalogue record for this book is available from the British Library

Made with paper from a sustainable forest

www.mileskelly.net
info@mileskelly.net

Junior
Encyclopedia

CONTENTS

INCREDIBLE SPACE 14-49

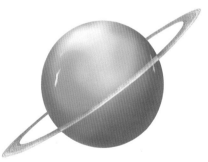

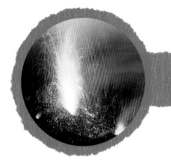

ACTIVE EARTH 52–81

WILD WEATHER 84–105

SUPER SCIENCE 108–137

DEADLY DINOSAURS 140–169

OCEAN LIFE 172–189

FANTASTIC MAMMALS
192–219

BRILLIANT BIRDS 222–249

AWESOME BUGS 252–281

ANCIENT EGYPT 284–313

ANCIENT ROME 316–343

KNIGHTS AND CASTLES
346–373

INCREDIBLE
SPACE

Space is everywhere

Space is all around Earth, high above the air.
Here on Earth's surface we are surrounded by
air. If you go upwards, up a mountain or in
an aircraft, air grows thinner until there
is none at all. This is where space begins.

Rocky ring
Asteroids are chunks of
rock, which are part of
our Solar System. They
circle the Sun in a ring,
between the planets
Mars and Jupiter. This is
called the asteroid belt.

Create your own space city

You will need
cardboard box • foil • scissors • glue
empty containers – plastic bottles, cardboard tubes,
cans, yoghurt pots and lids

1 Use the lid of the box as your base and cover it with foil. Cover all the empty containers with foil, too.

2 Cut plastic bottles to make domes. Use tubes and cans to make tunnels and passages, and lids to make satellite dishes.

3 Stick everything to the base and play with your own space city!

Astronauts are people who travel in space.

The surface of **Earth** is made up of land and sea.

Rockets are so powerful that they can launch spacecraft into space.

Our life-giving star

The Sun is our nearest star. It does not look like other stars because it is much closer to us. The Sun is not solid like Earth, but is a giant ball of super-hot gases.

The temperature of the Sun's surface is 6000 degrees Celsius

Sunspots are large, cool spots on the surface of the Sun

Prominences are huge loops of gas thrown out into space

Solar flares are explosions of energy that shoot out from the Sun

Ball of gas
The Sun's hot, glowing gas is always on the move, bubbling up to the surface and sinking back down again.

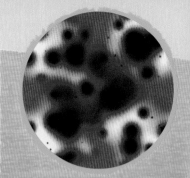

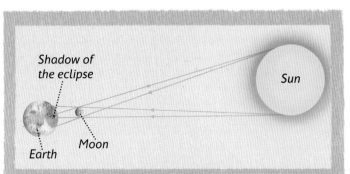

Shadow of
the eclipse

Sun

Earth

Moon

Solar eclipse

Every so often, the Sun, Moon and Earth line up in space so that the Moon is directly between Earth and the Sun. This stops sunlight from reaching a small area on Earth. The area grows dark and cold, as if night-time has come early. This is called an eclipse.

Sunspots are 1500 degrees cooler than the rest of the surface.

Solar prominences can be up to 100,000 kilometres long.

Blackout

When the Moon completely covers the Sun, it is called a total eclipse. All that can be seen is the Sun's corona, a ring of white glowing gas. Although the Moon and the Sun look the same size in an eclipse, the Sun is actually 400 times bigger than the Moon, and 400 times further away.

FUN FACT!

The surface of the Sun is nearly 60 times hotter than boiling water. It is so hot, it would melt a spacecraft that flew near it.

The planet family

The Sun is surrounded by a family of circling planets called the Solar System. This family is held together by an invisible force called gravity, which pulls things towards each other. It is the same force that pulls us to the ground and stops us floating away.

Big and small
The eight planets are all different. Mercury, nearest to the Sun, is small and hot. Venus, Earth and Mars are rocky and cooler. Beyond them Jupiter, Saturn, Uranus and Neptune are large and cold. Pluto is a tiny, icy dwarf planet.

Neptune

Saturn

Uranus

Pluto, dwarf planet

Held in place
The Sun's gravity pulls on the planets and keeps them travelling around it, in circles called orbits. Earth's gravity holds the Moon in its orbit.

Sun

Mercury

Moon

Jupiter

Venus

Earth

Mars

Some planets have **rings** made of ice, dust and rocks.

Some planets have **swirling atmospheres** of gas.

Make a mobile

You will need
card • scissors • colouring pencils • string
paper plate • sticky tape

1 Cut out nine circles of card, some big and some small, to be the planets and the Sun.

2 Colour the circles to look like the Sun and planets.

3 Use string and tape to hang the circles from the plate.

4 Hang your mobile from string stuck to the other side of the plate.

Earth in space

Earth moves through space at nearly 3000 metres a second. It weighs 6000 million, million, million tonnes. Up to two-thirds of the Earth's rocky surface is covered by water, making the seas and oceans.

Quiz time!

1 What is the Earth made up of?

2 What is the force that pulls us to the ground?

3 Who travels in space?

4 What is a star?

Q3 Picture clue

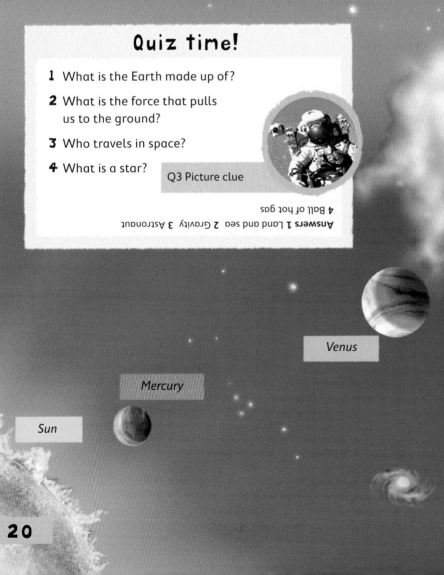

Answers 1 Land and sea **2** Gravity **3** Astronaut **4** Ball of hot gas

Venus

Mercury

Sun

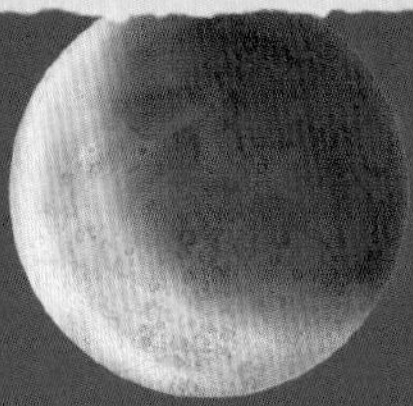

Moon

Earth

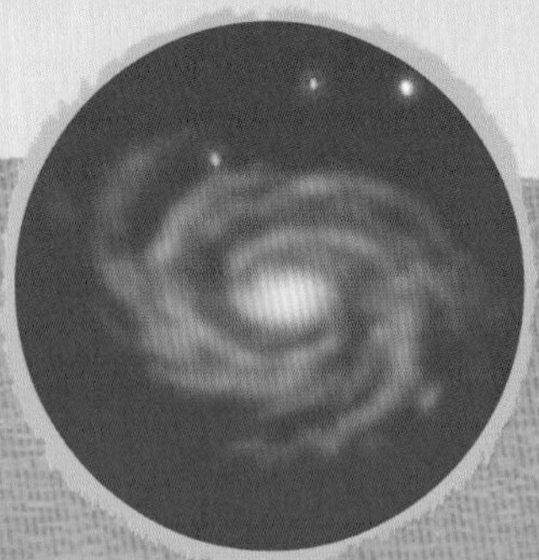

Galaxies are giant groups of millions or even trillions of stars.

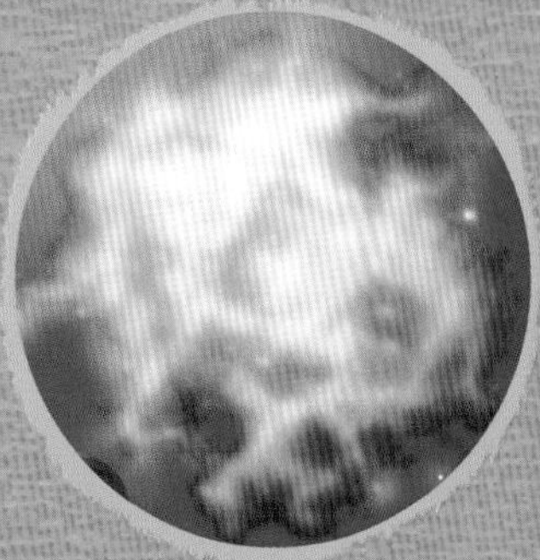

Bulging planet
Earth is the fifth largest planet in the Solar System. As it spins in space, Earth bulges in the middle, like a pumpkin.

A cloud of dust and gas in space is called a **nebula**.

Our atmosphere
Surrounding Earth is a layer of gases called the atmosphere. It stretches 700 kilometres from Earth's surface.

A **star** is a ball of very hot gas.

The Moon

Most planets have moons circling around them. Earth's Moon is one of the largest in the Solar System. Scientists think the Moon was formed over three billion years ago.

Circling Earth
The Moon is very close to Earth. It travels around Earth, taking one month to complete its journey.

Craters are made when rocks crash into the Moon's surface

Dark areas are low, flat plains called seas

Phases of the Moon

Over one month, the Moon changes from a thin crescent shape to a round shape. This is because as the Sun lights up one side of the Moon, the other side is dark. As the Moon circles the Earth, we see different parts of the lit side.

The Moon's surface can be seen in detail through a **telescope**.

3 Half Moon

4 Gibbous Moon

2 Crescent Moon

1 New Moon

5 Full Moon

8 Crescent Moon

6 Gibbous Moon

7 Half Moon

The **far side of the Moon** always faces away from Earth. The near side always turns towards Earth.

Surface of the Moon

The Moon is a dry, dusty ball of rock. Its surface is covered in hollows called craters.

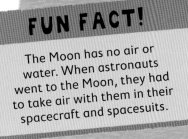

FUN FACT!

The Moon has no air or water. When astronauts went to the Moon, they had to take air with them in their spacecraft and spacesuits.

Earth's neighbours

Venus and Mars are the nearest planets to Earth. Venus is closer to the Sun than Earth, and Mars is further away. The time it takes for a planet to circle the Sun is called a year. A year on Venus is **225** days, on Earth **365** days, and on Mars **687** days.

Red desert
Mars is very dry, like a desert, and covered in red dust. Winds on Mars whip up huge dust storms that can cover the whole planet.

Valles Marineris is an enormous valley that cuts across Mars

Olympus Mons is the largest volcano on Mars

The white ice caps are made of frozen carbon dioxide gas

Mars

24

Bright in the sky
Venus shines like a star in the sky because its atmosphere reflects sunlight so well.

Rocky surface

Venus has a volcano called **Maat Mons**. It is 6 kilometres high.

Mars has two small moons. **Phobos** is only 27 kilometres across.

Venus

Poisonous clouds with drops of acid

Planet spotting

See if you can spot Venus in the night sky. It is often the first bright star to appear in the evening, just above where the Sun has set. Sometimes it is called the evening star.

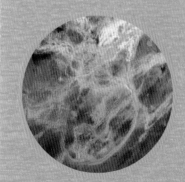

Venus is the **hottest** planet because its clouds trap the heat.

Tiny planets

Pluto is a dwarf planet – smaller than the Moon. It is so tiny and far away that it was not discovered until 1930. Mercury looks like the Moon. It is a cratered ball of rock. It has no atmosphere, so the sunny side is boiling hot, while the other side is freezing cold.

Pluto's moon
If you were on Pluto, its moon Charon would look much larger than Earth's Moon because Charon is very close to Pluto.

The cratered surface of Pluto is covered in solid ice

Sunlit side

Pluto

Make craters

You will need
flour • tray • marble or stone

1. Spread some flour about 2 centimetres deep in a tray and smooth over the surface.

2. Drop a marble or stone onto the flour and see the saucer-shaped crater that it makes.

Pluto's moon, **Charon,** was only discovered in 1976.

The **Sun** looks huge as it rises over Mercury.

Planet of craters

Mercury has many craters. This shows how often it was hit by space rocks. One was so large, it shattered rocks on the other side of the planet.

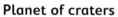

Caloris Basin is a large crater

The dusty surface is covered in craters

Mercury

FUN FACT!

There are two other dwarf planets called Ceres and Eris.

Massive planets

Jupiter is the largest planet in the Solar System. It is 11 times wider than Earth, although it is still much smaller than the Sun. Saturn, the next largest planet, is more than nine times as wide as Earth.

Jupiter

Stormy surface
There are many storms on Jupiter, but none as large or long lasting as the Great Red Spot.

The Great Red Spot is a 300-year-old storm

Different-coloured clouds stretch around Jupiter

Jupiter has a moon called **Io**. It has many active volcanoes.

Saturn's rings

Although Saturn's rings are very wide, they stretch out in a very thin layer around the planet.

Saturn

Yellow clouds stretch to make faint bands

The **Galilean moons** are Jupiter's four biggest moons. They were discovered by Italian astronomer Galileo Galilei.

FUN FACT!

Saturn is the lightest planet in the Solar System. It would float like a cork in water.

Saturn's shining rings are made of millions of chunks of ice

Distant giant
From Earth, Saturn looks like a faint but bright-yellow star in the sky.

Far, far away

Uranus and Neptune are gas giants like Jupiter and Saturn. They are the next two planets beyond Saturn but much smaller — less than half as wide. Their surfaces are made of liquid and gas.

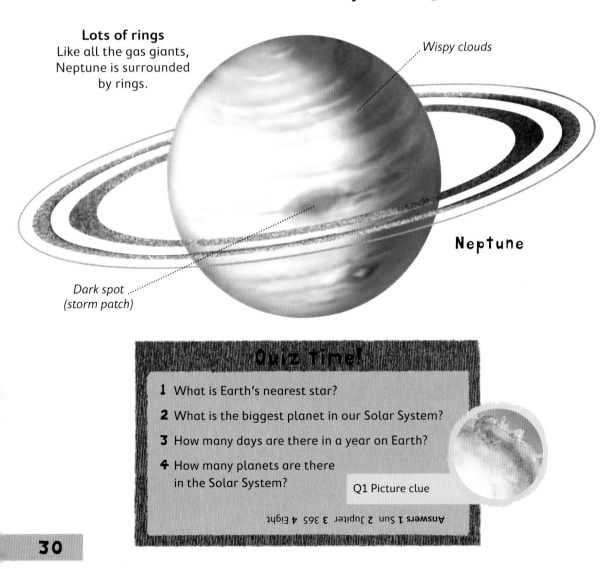

Lots of rings
Like all the gas giants, Neptune is surrounded by rings.

Wispy clouds

Dark spot (storm patch)

Neptune

Quiz Time!

1 What is Earth's nearest star?

2 What is the biggest planet in our Solar System?

3 How many days are there in a year on Earth?

4 How many planets are there in the Solar System?

Q1 Picture clue

Answers 1 Sun 2 Jupiter 3 365 4 Eight

Covered with clouds

Uranus

Rings of ice and dust

Neptune's rings are thinner and darker than Saturn's.

Sideways spin
Most planets spin upright, but Uranus spins on its side. It may have been knocked over when something crashed into it millions of years ago.

Neptune's **bright blue clouds** make the whole planet look blue.

Miranda   Ariel   Umbriel

Titania   Oberon

Many moons
Uranus has five moons. Oberon is the second largest moon. It has lots of craters, but also has a mountain about 6.5 kilometres tall.

FUN FACT!
Uranus is very cold because it is so far from the Sun.

31

Birth of a star

A star is born in clouds of dust and gas called nebulae. These clouds look like shining patches in the night sky. They shrink as gravity pulls the dust and gas together. At the centre, the gas gets hotter until a new star is born.

Learning about stars
Stars are born and die across the Universe all the time. By looking at stars in the different stages of their lives, astonomers have learned how they work.

1 Clumps of gas in the nebula start to shrink into tight balls that will become stars

2 The gas spirals as it is pulled inwards. Any leftover gas and dust may form planets around the new star

Quiz time!

1 What are Saturn's rings made of?

2 What is the name of the biggest volcano on Mars?

3 When was Pluto's moon Charon discovered?

4 How old is the Sun?

Q1 Picture clue

4 Five billion years old

Answers 1 Chunks of ice **2** Olympus Mons **3** 1976

Large **white stars** make energy very quickly and burn brightly.

Small **red stars** are cooler and shine less brightly.

3 Deep in its centre, the new star starts making energy, but it is still hidden by the cloud of dust and gas

4 The dust and gas are blown away and the star shines

The Sun has existed for five billion years — only half its life.

The Milky Way

The Sun is part of a huge family of stars called the Milky Way galaxy. There are billions of other stars in the galaxy and there are also billions of galaxies outside the Milky Way.

Our galaxy
The arms at the edge of the Milky Way contain young, bright stars. The centre of the Milky Way is made of dust and gas.

Irregular galaxies don't have a particular shape.

Collision!

Galaxies sometimes get so close to each another that they collide. When this happens, they may pull each other out of shape, or merge into one larger galaxy.

Spiral galaxies have arms made of bright stars.

FUN FACT!

Our galaxy is called the Milky Way because it looks like a faint band of light in the sky, as though milk has been split across space.

Elliptical galaxies are shaped like a huge squashed ball.

Exploring the sky

Outlines of people and animals in star patterns in the sky are called constellations. Astronomers named the constellations to help them find their way around the skies.

Northern Hemisphere

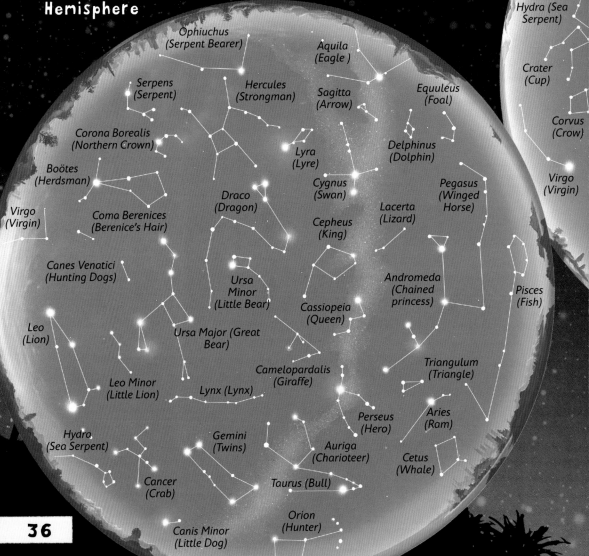

Sextans (Sextant)

Hydra (Sea Serpent)

Crater (Cup)

Corvus (Crow)

Virgo (Virgin)

Ophiuchus (Serpent Bearer)

Aquila (Eagle)

Serpens (Serpent)

Hercules (Strongman)

Sagitta (Arrow)

Equuleus (Foal)

Corona Borealis (Northern Crown)

Lyra (Lyre)

Delphinus (Dolphin)

Boötes (Herdsman)

Cygnus (Swan)

Pegasus (Winged Horse)

Draco (Dragon)

Lacerta (Lizard)

Virgo (Virgin)

Coma Berenices (Berenice's Hair)

Cepheus (King)

Canes Venatici (Hunting Dogs)

Ursa Minor (Little Bear)

Cassiopeia (Queen)

Andromeda (Chained princess)

Pisces (Fish)

Leo (Lion)

Ursa Major (Great Bear)

Triangulum (Triangle)

Leo Minor (Little Lion)

Lynx (Lynx)

Camelopardalis (Giraffe)

Perseus (Hero)

Aries (Ram)

Hydra (Sea Serpent)

Gemini (Twins)

Auriga (Charioteer)

Cetus (Whale)

Cancer (Crab)

Taurus (Bull)

Orion (Hunter)

Canis Minor (Little Dog)

Lepus
(Hare)

Canis Major
(Great Dog)

Columba
(Dove)

Eridanus
(River Eridanus)

Puppis (Stern), Carina
(Keel) and Vela (Sail)

Caelum
(Chisel)

Fornax
(Furnace)

Pictor
(Easel)

Dorado
(Goldfish)

Cetus
(Whale)

Reticulum
(Net)

Volans (Flying
Fish)

Phoenix
(Phoenix)

Crux
(Southern
Cross)

Chamaeleon
(Chameleon)

Grus (Crane), Tucana
(Toucan) and Pavo
(Peacock)

Musca
(Fly)

Apus (Bird of
Paradise)

Centaurus
(Centaur)

Triangulum Australe
(Southern Triangle)

Indus
(Indian)

Piscis
Austrinus
(Southern
Fish)

Ara (Altar)

Libra
(Scales)

Corona
Australis
(Southern
Crown)

Aquarius
(Water
Carrier)

Scorpius
(Scorpion)

Sagittarius
(Archer)

Capricornus
(Sea Goat)

Serpens (Serpent) and
Ophiuchus (Serpent
Bearer)

Southern
Hemisphere

The **Scorpion** is so-called because it looks like a scorpion.

The **Great Bear** is one of the best-known star formations.

In the North
If you live North of the Equator (the imaginary line through the centre of Earth), these are the constellations that you can see at night.

In the South
If you live south of the Equator, you can see a different set of constellations in the sky, including the Great Dog.

The **Southern Cross** can be used as a compass.

Launching into space

To blast into space, a rocket has to
travel nearly 40 times faster
than a jumbo jet. If it goes
any slower, gravity pulls it
back to Earth. Rockets are
powered by burning fuel.

Blast off!
The space shuttle takes
off from Earth as a rocket.
It is blasted into space by
three rocket engines and
two huge booster engines.

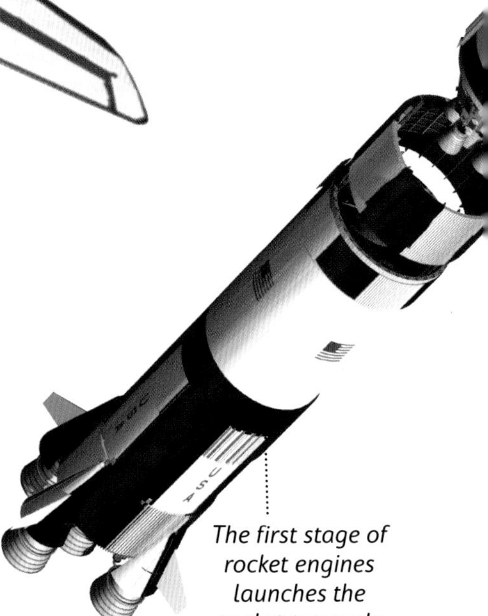

*The first stage of
rocket engines
launches the
rocket upwards*

Ready for space

One rocket isn't powerful enough to launch a spacecraft into space. Rockets have two or three stages, which are really separate rocket engines on top of each other.

The third stage takes the spacecraft into space

The second stage begins when the fuel from the first rocket stage is used up

The spacecraft carried by a rocket is called its **'payload'**.

Make a rocket

You will need
sheet of card • cardboard tube
sticky tape • scissors

1 Use the tube for the main body of the rocket. Make a cone shape with some of the card and stick it to one end.

2 In a safe place, 'launch' the rocket by throwing it up at an angle. It should tumble out of control.

3 Add fins by sticking four large, card triangles to the base. Now it should fly much straighter.

Different-sized rockets are used for different-sized spacecraft.

Life in space

Space is a dangerous place for astronauts.
It can be boiling hot in the sunshine or
freezing in Earth's shadow. Dust and rocks
that speed through space could make
a small hole in a spacecraft,
letting the air leak out.

Protective suit
Spacesuits protect
astronauts and carry vital
equipment. The suits have
many layers to make them
strong. They also hold the
air that astronauts need
to breathe.

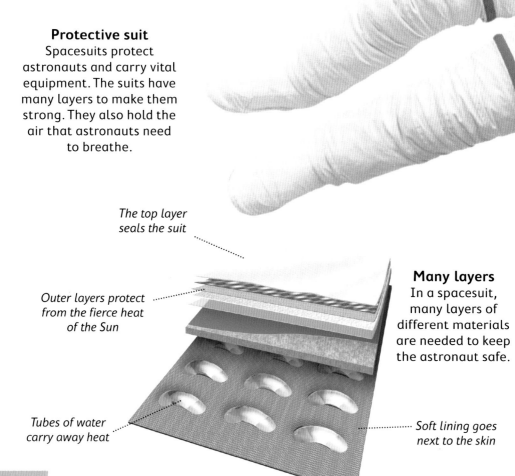

*The top layer
seals the suit*

*Outer layers protect
from the fierce heat
of the Sun*

Many layers
In a spacesuit,
many layers of
different materials
are needed to keep
the astronaut safe.

*Tubes of water
carry away heat*

*Soft lining goes
next to the skin*

The **visor** protects the astronaut's face from sunlight.

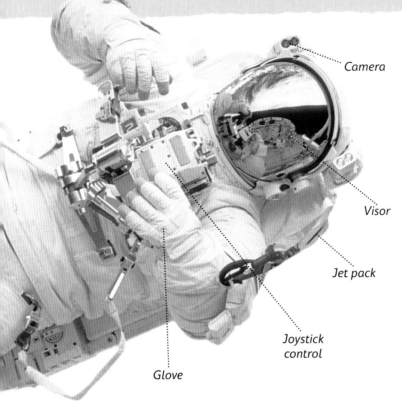

Camera

Visor

Jet pack

Joystick control

Glove

The **joystick** lets the astronaut move around in space.

Moon landing

On 20 July 1969, American astronauts Neil Armstrong and Buzz Aldrin became the first humans on the Moon.

Sleeping bags are fixed to a wall in the spacecraft to stop them from floating away.

At home in space

A space station is a home in space for astronauts. It has a kitchen, cabins with sleeping bags, toilets, washbasins and sometimes showers. There are also places to work and controls where astronauts can check that everything is working properly.

Building the ISS
The International Space Station is the only base in space. It was built in space using different pieces. The first piece was launched in 1998.

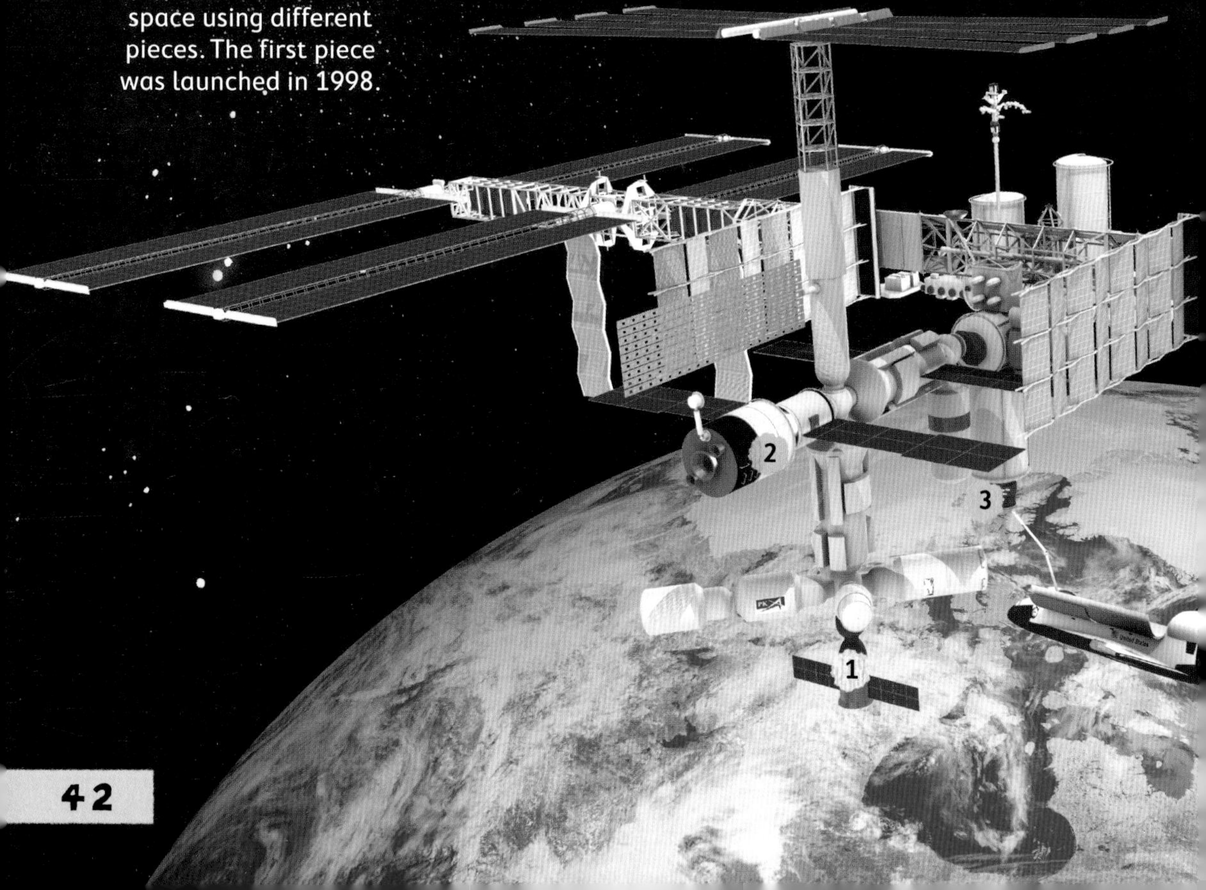

1

2

3

Key

1 Soyuz spacecraft transports astronauts to and from the ISS

2 Astronauts sleep inside the living module

3 Visiting spacecraft join the ISS at docking ports

4 Solar panels always point towards the Sun

FUN FACT!

The US space station Skylab, launched in 1973, fell back to Earth in 1979. Most of it landed in the ocean but some pieces hit Australia.

Living in space
There are six astronauts on board the ISS. They carry out important research about space and test equipment.

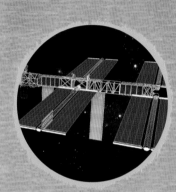

Solar panels use sunlight to make electricity for the ISS.

The ISS can leave a trail of light across the sky.

4

Exploring with robots

Robotic spacecraft called probes have explored
all the planets. Probes travel in space to take
measurements and close-up pictures. They send
the information back to scientists on Earth.
Some probes circle planets taking pictures. For
a close-up look, a probe can land on the surface.

Exploring Mars

Mars Pathfinder carried a small rover called Sojourner to Mars in 1997. Sojourner spent three months on Mars, testing the soil and rocks.

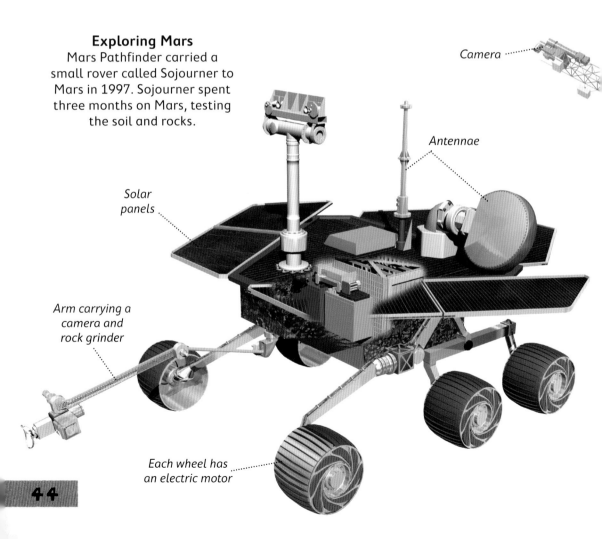

Camera

Antennae

Solar panels

Arm carrying a camera and rock grinder

Each wheel has an electric motor

INCREDIBLE SPACE

Journey to the giants
Two Voyager probes left Earth in 1977 to visit the four gas giants. They sent back thousands of pictures of the planets.

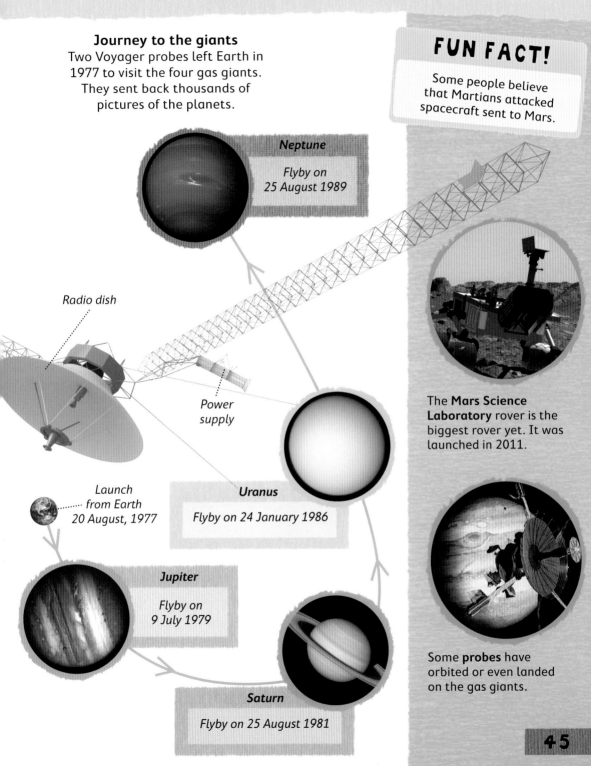

Neptune

Flyby on
25 August 1989

Radio dish

Power
supply

Launch
from Earth
20 August, 1977

Uranus

Flyby on 24 January 1986

Jupiter

Flyby on
9 July 1979

Saturn

Flyby on 25 August 1981

FUN FACT!
Some people believe that Martians attacked spacecraft sent to Mars.

The **Mars Science Laboratory** rover is the biggest rover yet. It was launched in 2011.

Some **probes** have orbited or even landed on the gas giants.

Spies in space

Hundreds of satellites circle the Earth in space. They are used for communication, checking the weather, making maps and finding out more about space.

Making connections
Communication satellites can beam pictures directly to your home through an aerial dish.

Weather watchers
Weather satellites look down at the clouds and give warnings when a violent storm is approaching.

FUN FACT!

Spy satellites circling Earth take pictures of secret locations and listen to secret radio messages from military ships or aircraft.

Deep in space
Special satellite telescopes let astronomers look far out into the Universe to discover what is there.

On the look-out
Earth-watching satellites look out for pollution, such as dirty air over cities.

Satellites can spot icebergs that may be a danger to ships.

Some satellites provide information that helps people **navigate**, or find their way around.

Off to the Moon

The first men landed on the Moon in 1969. Three astronauts went into space on the US *Apollo 11* mission. Neil Armstrong was the first person to walk on the Moon. Only five other Apollo missions have landed on the Moon since then.

Going the distance
The distance from Earth to the Moon is nearly 400,000 kilometres. That is about as far as travelling round Earth ten times.

Command Module

Lunar Module

Legs folded for the journey

Men on the Moon

The *Apollo 11* astronauts stayed on the Moon for three days to explore and carry out experiments.

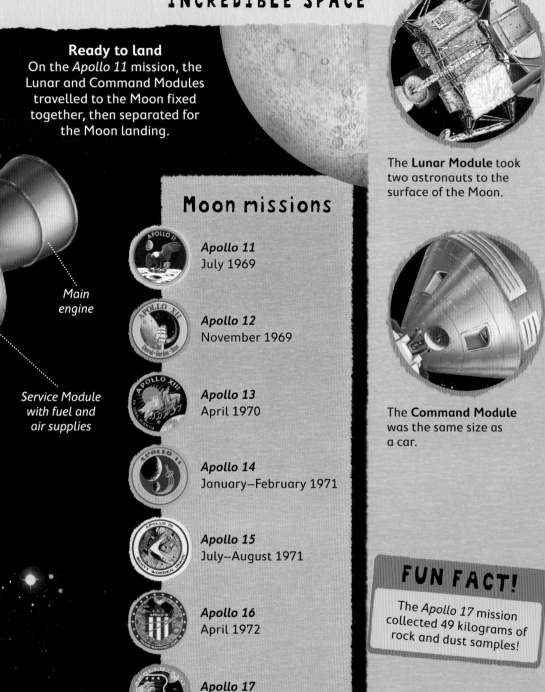

Ready to land
On the *Apollo 11* mission, the Lunar and Command Modules travelled to the Moon fixed together, then separated for the Moon landing.

The **Lunar Module** took two astronauts to the surface of the Moon.

Main engine

Service Module with fuel and air supplies

The **Command Module** was the same size as a car.

Moon missions

Apollo 11
July 1969

Apollo 12
November 1969

Apollo 13
April 1970

Apollo 14
January–February 1971

Apollo 15
July–August 1971

Apollo 16
April 1972

Apollo 17
December 1972

FUN FACT!
The *Apollo 17* mission collected 49 kilograms of rock and dust samples!

ACTIVE EARTH

How Earth was made

When an old star explodes, the remains create clouds of gas and dust. In these clouds, new stars and planets form. Earth came from a huge cloud of gas and dust about 4500 million years ago.

The birth of Earth

A star exploded near a cloud of gas and dust, making the cloud spin. Gases gathered at the centre of the cloud, forming the Sun. Rocks crashed into each other, creating the planets. Earth is one of these planets.

1 *A cloud of gas and dust started to spin*

2 *Dust gathered into lumps of rock, creating planets including Earth*

3 *Earth began to spin and formed a hard shell*

5 Earth was first made up of one piece of land, but it has now split into seven chunks called continents

FUN FACT!

Millions of rocks crash into Earth's atmosphere as it speeds through space. Large rocks that reach the ground are called meteorites.

The surfaces of Earth and the **Moon** were hit by rocks, making hollows called craters.

4 Volcanoes erupted and released gases, forming the first atmosphere

NORTH AMERICA

EUROPE

ASIA

AFRICA

SOUTH AMERICA

OCEANIA

ANTARCTICA

Continents

There are seven continents in the world. Asia is the largest continent and Oceania is the smallest.

Meteor Crater is near Arizona, USA. It is 1200 metres wide and 170 metres deep.

53

Inside Earth

Earth is made up of many different layers.
We live on the outer layer — the thin, rocky
crust that is covered with land and water.

The layers of Earth
As well as the crust, Earth has a solid
mantle and a core. The outer part of
the core is liquid, but the inner core
is made of solid metal.

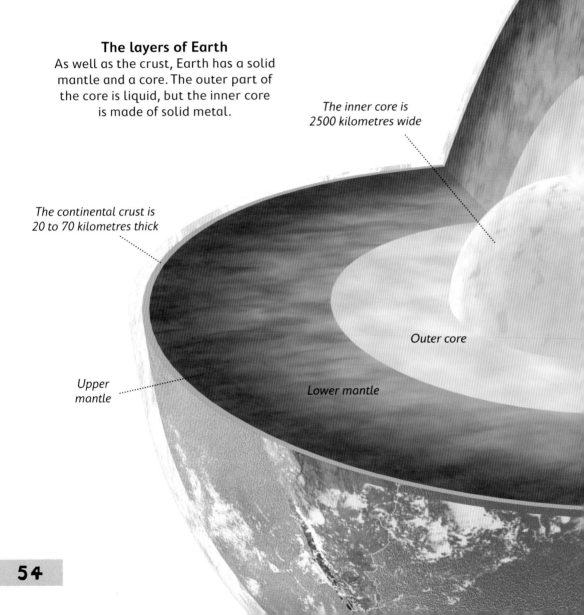

*The inner core is
2500 kilometres wide*

*The continental crust is
20 to 70 kilometres thick*

Outer core

*Upper
mantle*

Lower mantle

The crust is divided into chunks of rock called plates

Atmosphere

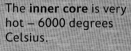

The **inner core** is very hot – 6000 degrees Celsius.

Molten rock can burst through the crust, creating volcanoes.

Earth's surface is mainly made of a rock called **granite**.

Quiz time!

1 How many continents are there?

2 What helped form Earth's atmosphere?

3 What are rocks from space that hit Earth called?

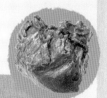

Q3 Picture clue

Answers 1 Seven 2 Erupting volcanoes 3 Meteorites

Days and years

Earth is like a huge spinning top that leans to one side. It continues to spin because it was formed by a spinning cloud of gas.

Afternoon

A day on Earth
Earth takes 24 hours to spin around once. This period of time is called a day.

Day and night
It is daytime when one part of Earth faces the Sun. At the same time on the opposite side of Earth, it is night-time.

Evening

Make a spinning globe

You will need
globe • torch

1 In a darkened room, shine the torch at your globe. The side facing the torch (or Sun) is lit up, so there it is daytime. On the dark side of the globe, it is night-time.

2 If you slowly spin the globe, you will see how daylight moves around Earth.

N

S

A year on Earth
Earth moves around the Sun in a path called an orbit. It takes one year to make this journey. In that time it spins just over 365 times.

Earth spins around two points – the **North and South poles**.

Morning

Sun

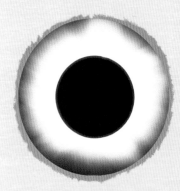

When the Sun, Earth and Moon line up, it is called an **eclipse**.

The **Sun's rays** take about 8 minutes and 20 seconds to reach Earth.

Night

57

Changing rocks

When rocks form in Earth's crust, they can change. This happens in two ways. Sometimes the rock is heated by hot rocks moving up through the crust. Other times, the crust is squashed and heated, and mountains form.

Wind and rain can wear away the rock's surface

The rock cycle
The movement of rocks from the surface to underground and back again is called the rock cycle. Rocks are often changed during this journey.

58

Breccia is made of rocks held together with natural cements.

Quiz time!

1 What is the centre of Earth called?

2 How thick is Earth's crust?

3 When the Sun, Moon and Earth line up, what is it called?

4 How hot is the Sun's core?

Q3 Picture clue

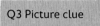

Answers **1** Core **2** 20 to 70 kilometres **3** Eclipse **4** 6000 degrees Celsius

Limestone is white, yellow or greyish in colour. It is a soft rock.

Hot rock travels to the surface through the pipe in a volcano

Rock can become squashed, causing it to fold together

Chalk is a soft rock that formed millions of years ago.

Rock melts, forming hot, liquid rock called magma

Violent volcanoes

Volcanoes occur when hot, liquid rock shoots up through Earth's surface. Beneath a volcano is a huge space filled with molten (liquid) rock. This is the magma chamber. Eruptions happen when pressure builds up inside the chamber.

Volcanic explosion
When a volcano erupts, the hot rock from inside Earth escapes as ash, smoke, flying lava bombs and rivers of lava.

Lava bomb

Layers of rock from previous eruptions

Make an erupting volcano

You will need
bicarbonate of soda • plastic bottle
red food colouring • vinegar • sand • tray

1 Put a tablespoon of bicarbonate of soda in the plastic bottle.

2 Stand the bottle on a tray and make a cone of sand around it.

3 Put a few drops of red food colouring in half a cup of vinegar.

4 Pour the vinegar into the bottle and watch your volcano erupt!

Shield volcanoes form when lava flows from the vent creating a dome shape.

Ash and smoke

Lava flowing away from vent

Main vent

Cone-shaped volcanoes form when ash settles on thick lava.

Magma chamber beneath the volcano

Crater volcanoes form when cone-shaped volcanoes sink into magma chambers.

Making mountains

It takes millions of years for mountains to form. Young mountains are the highest, but the peaks are made of soft rocks so they break down easily. Underneath are harder rocks that wear away over a longer period of time.

Mountain range is pushed up

Active volcano

Volcanic mountains
These mountains are formed when lava erupts through Earth's crust. As the lava cools, it creates a rocky layer.

Molten (liquid) rock

Fold mountains
When plates in Earth's crust crash together, rock is pushed up, forming mountains.

Highest peaks
Some mountaintops are so high that they sit above the clouds.

Some **mountain peaks** are covered in snow.

Folded and uplifted rock

Block of rock forced up

Mountaineers are people who like to climb mountains.

Block mountains
Sometimes, Earth's crust splits and cracks. Blocks of rock are then pushed up through these cracks.

FUN FACT!
The highest mountain in the world is Mount Everest, which is part of the Himalayas. It is 8848 metres tall.

Extreme earthquakes

An earthquake is caused by movements in Earth's crust. It starts deep underground at the focus. Shockwaves move from the focus in all directions, shaking the rock. The quake is strongest at the epicentre.

Locking plates

Earth's crust is made of plates and some of them have jagged edges. Sometimes they lock together – when they suddenly unlock, it can cause an earthquake.

The fault line is where two plates rub together

Tsunami hits

As the giant wave moves into shallow water near the coast, it becomes taller. It then crashes onto the shore, flooding the land.

A **fault line** can be made up of narrow cracks or deep canyons.

The epicentre is where the shockwaves reach the surface, directly above the focus

Shockwaves from an earthquake can create a giant wave at sea called a tsunami

The force of an earthquake is measured using the **Richter scale**. At level 7, buildings collapse and cities can be destroyed.

FUN FACT!

The biggest earthquake ever recorded was near Valdivia, Chile, in May 1960. It measured 9.5 on the Richter scale.

The focus is deep underground – this is where the earthquake starts

Lakes and rivers

A mighty river can start from a small spring,
where water flows from the ground. The trickle
of water from a spring is called a stream. When
streams join together, they make a river.

A river's journey
High in the mountains, streams
begin to form a river. The river
then flows through the
mountains towards the sea.

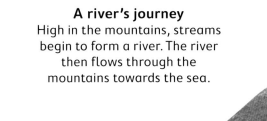

Delta
A group of sandy
islands at the mouth
of a river.

Stream
A small river of water that comes from a spring.

FUN FACT!

Most lakes are blue, but some are green, pink, red or even white. The colours are made by tiny creatures called algae or by minerals in the water.

A **waterfall** forms when a river flows over a ledge.

Meander
A bend in a river as it winds down to the sea.

A **lake** is a large body of water surrounded by land.

Oxbow lake
A lake that forms when meanders separate from the main river.

Caves and chambers

Rocks can be worn away by rainwater
trickling into tiny cracks and crevices.
Over millions of years, this creates caves,
chambers and waterfalls underground.

Stalactites and stalagmites

Stalagmites grow up from the
floor of caves and stalactites grow
down from the roof. Over time,
they can join together. They are
made of the minerals in water.

Dissolving rock

Rainwater contains chemicals that can turn it into a weak acid. Acidic rainwater can slowly dissolve rock, especially limestone, when it trickles through any cracks.

FUN FACT!

The largest cave in the world is the Sarawak Chamber in Malaysia. At 600 metres long and 400 metres wide, you could fit eight Boeing 747 aeroplanes inside it.

Waterfall in a shaft (vertical cave)

Gallery (horizontal cave)

Stalactites

Stalagmites

Caves have been discovered full of **crystals**. The crystals are made of minerals.

Some spectacular **cave formations** are thousands of years old.

Dry deserts

The driest places on Earth are deserts.
In many deserts there is a short period
of rain every year, but some have
dry weather for many years.

Polar deserts

Antarctica is a polar desert. There is hardly
any rain and the warmest temperature is
less than 10 degrees Celsius.

Masses of sand

There are six main deserts in the world. The largest is the Sahara in Africa. It is made up of sand, pebbles and boulders. Some deserts have oases – freshwater springs that flow out of the ground.

Ridges of sand are blown by strong winds into dunes.

Camels have broad feet that stop them sinking in the sand.

Deserts around the world

1 Great Basin and Mojave
2 Atacama
3 Sahara
4 Arabian
5 Gobi
6 Great Sandy, Gibson, Great Victoria, Simpson

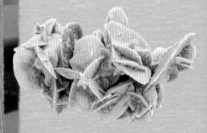

Desert roses are formed when sand joins with minerals.

Forests of the world

There are three main types of forest –
coniferous, temperate and rainforest.
In coniferous forests, the trees stay in
leaf all year round. In temperate woodland,
deciduous trees lose their leaves in winter.

Wet forests

In rainforests, large numbers of
trees and plants grow close together.
It rains almost every day. The vegetation
is so thick, it can take a raindrop
ten minutes to fall to the ground.

Autumn leaves

In deciduous forests, the leaves turn orange,
yellow and brown as they start to drop in
autumn. New leaves grow in spring.

Toucan

Perfect habitat
Trees provide homes, or habitats, for millions of animals and plants.

The **Amazon rainforest** is the largest tropical rainforest in the world.

Squirrels live in both temperate and coniferous forests.

Quiz time!

Can you guess what these woodland creatures are?

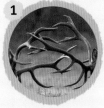
1

2

3

Answers 1 Deer 2 Red panda 3 Woodpecker

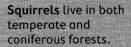

The **redwood** is the tallest tree in the world – more than 100 metres in height.

Water, water everywhere

Oceans cover more than two-thirds of Earth's rocky surface. Their total area is about 362 million square kilometres, which means there is more than twice as much ocean than land!

ARCTIC OCEAN

The Mediterranean Sea borders Spain and France.

Bering Sea

PACIFIC OCEAN

Mediterranean Sea

ATLANTIC OCEAN

Caribbean Sea

The Caribbean Sea is part of the Atlantic Ocean.

Main oceans

Although all the oceans flow into each other, we know them as five different oceans – the Pacific, Atlantic, Indian, Southern and Arctic. Each ocean is made up of smaller areas of water called seas.

74

FUN FACT!

The average depth of the Pacific is more than 4000 metres, making it the world's deepest ocean.

Hydrothermal vents are underwater chimneys that spurt hot water and minerals.

Many cities such as Kuwait sit on the Persian Gulf, which is part of the Arabian Sea.

Ocean waves carve rocks into amazing shapes such as **sea stacks**.

Arabian
Sea

South
China
Sea

PACIFIC
OCEAN

INDIAN
OCEAN

Icebergs break away from huge glaciers and then drift and melt into the ocean.

SOUTHERN
OCEAN

75

Under the ocean

There are plains, mountains and valleys
under the ocean in areas called basins.
As the ocean floor is slowly moving,
its features are always changing.

Volcanic island

Volcanic islands

In the ocean, volcanoes may grow tall
enough, over many eruptions, to break
the water's surface as islands.

Hill

Ocean trench
(deep valley)

Land

A rim is a flat continental shelf that meets the shore

Types of reef

1

A **coral reef** may build up around a volcanic island.

2

When a volcanic island sinks, it leaves a **lagoon** – water that is separate from the main ocean.

A continental slope is the side that drops away from the shelf

Spreading ridge

Hills and valleys
Under the ocean there is a landscape similar to that found on land. There are flat plains, steep hills, huge underwater volcanoes and deep valleys.

3

An **atoll** is the ring of coral reef surrounding the lagoon.

77

Rivers of ice

Glaciers are huge areas of ice that form near mountaintops. They slide slowly down the mountainside and melt. As a glacier moves, some rocks break off and are carried along.

Area where the glacier forms

Cracks in the ice

Melting ice

The end of a glacier is called the 'snout'. This is where the ice starts to melt, causing large chunks called icebergs to break off into the ocean.

Make an iceberg

You will need
plastic container • clear bowl • water

1 Fill the container with water and put it in the freezer until it is frozen. This is your iceberg.

2 Remove the iceberg from the container. Fill the clear bowl with water and add your iceberg.

3 Look through the side of the container to see how much of your iceberg is underwater and what shape it makes.

Beautiful **U-shaped valleys** were created by glaciers.

Glacier valleys
Glaciers have helped to shape Earth. As a glacier flows down a mountain, the heavy ice pushes and scrapes the soil and rocks. This carves a huge U-shaped valley.

Glacial ice melts and crashes into the sea.

Snout

Mushroom stones can be formed when glaciers cut away the bottom part of the rock.

Melted ice, called meltwater, can be as small as a puddle or as big as a lake

Coral reef life

Huge underwater walls are built up from coral –
the leftover skeletons of sea creatures called
polyps. Over millions of years, enough skeletons
pile up to form huge structures called reefs.
Coral reefs are full of sea life.

Camouflage colours
The creatures found in coral reefs are
very colourful. This helps them to blend
in with their surroundings, making it
difficult for hunters to spot them.

Life in coral reefs

1 Sea horse
2 Parrot fish
3 Giant clam
4 Butterfly fish
5 Staghorn coral
6 Clownfish
7 Sea anemone
8 Lion fish
9 Tube sponge
10 Soft tree coral
11 Cleaner wrasse fish
12 Sea slug
13 Brain coral
14 Stone fish
15 Cup coral

There are many different **shapes** and **colours** of coral.

The largest coral reef in the world is the **Great Barrier Reef**, off the coast of Australia.

Hawksbill sea turtles can be found in coral reefs, feeding on sea sponges.

WILD
WEATHER

The atmosphere

Our planet is wrapped in a blanket of air called the atmosphere. It stretches for hundreds of kilometres above our heads. Without an atmosphere, there would be no weather.

Earth from above

The atmosphere keeps in heat, especially at night when part of the planet faces away from the Sun. During the day, it becomes a sunscreen instead.

Oxygen to breathe
The higher up you go, the less oxygen there is in the air. We need oxygen to breathe, so mountaineers often wear special breathing equipment.

Layers of air
The atmosphere stretches right into space. Scientists have split it into five layers, or spheres.

Low-level satellites orbit within the outer layers of the atmosphere.

Exosphere
190 to 960 kilometres

Thermosphere
80 to 190 kilometres

Meteorites are pieces of rock from space that fall through the atmosphere to Earth's surface.

Mesosphere
50 to 80 kilometres

Stratosphere
10 to 50 kilometres

Aeroplanes fly just above the clouds, where the air is thinner.

Troposphere
0 to 10 kilometres

What is weather?

Rain, sunshine and snow are all types of weather. In parts of the world, such as near the Equator, the weather is nearly always the same. Most of the world has a temperate climate, meaning the weather changes daily.

The world's climates
The coloured rings show the different climates around the world. In general, the warmest climates are found close to the Equator.

North Pole

Desert

Mountainous

Tropical forest

South Pole

86

Polar climates

The coldest climates in the world are found at the North and South poles. They are furthest from the Equator, and so it is cold and icy all year round.

Rainforests are very hot but they also have daily downpours of rain.

Tropical grassland

Temperate grassland

Polar

Mountains can be very cold and covered in snow.

Equator

Wet temperate

Cold temperate

Dry temperate

Deserts are home to many plants and animals, such as lizards, that can survive in the heat.

Forecasting the weather

Working out what the weather will be like is called forecasting. By looking at changes in the atmosphere, and comparing them to weather patterns of the past, forecasters can say what the weather may be like in the future.

Weather maps
Weather scientists called meteorologists plot their findings on maps called synoptic charts.

Black lines with red semi-circles and blue triangles are where a cold front meets a warm front

White lines are isobars – closely spaced isobars mean strong wind

A warm front (where warm air pushes over colder air) is shown by a red semi-circle

A cold front (where cold air pushes under warm air) is shown by a blue triangle

Weather Symbols

Make your own synoptic chart. Here are some symbols to get you started. Can you guess what they mean?

1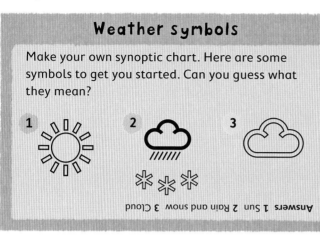

2

3

Answers **1** Sun **2** Rain and snow **3** Cloud

A **warm front** is a sign of cooler weather to come.

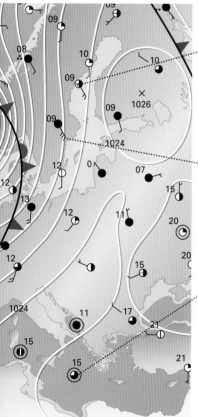

The white semi-circle shows how much cloud cover there is

The three lines on the tail show that the wind is very strong

This symbol shows an area of calm, with lots of cloud cover

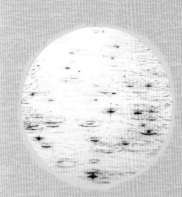

A **cold front** can bring thunderstorms and heavy rain.

Meteorologists use **weather stations** to collect information about the weather.

All the seasons

The seasons are caused by Earth's movement around the Sun. It takes one year for Earth to orbit the Sun. Earth is tilted, so over the year the North and South poles take turns facing towards the Sun, giving us seasons.

Spring in the Northern Hemisphere (March–May)
The temperature begins to get warmer. Flowers bloom, and trees start to grow their leaves again.

N

S

Sun

Summer in the Northern Hemisphere (June–September)
In June, the North Pole leans towards the Sun. The Sun heats the northern half of Earth, making it summertime.

N

S

In **summer**, people like to enjoy the sunshine by going to the beach.

Sunshine at midnight

At the North Pole during the height of summer, the Sun never disappears below the horizon.

In **winter**, many people go skiing and snowboarding in the snow.

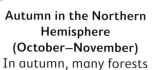

Winter in the Northern Hemisphere (December–March)
In December, the North Pole leans away from the Sun, meaning it is winter.

FUN FACT!

In Stockholm, Sweden, the longest day lasts 21 hours because the Sun disappears below the horizon for only three hours!

Autumn in the Northern Hemisphere (October–November)
In autumn, many forests change colour, from green to golden brown. Trees prepare for winter by losing their leaves.

Tropical seasons

The tropics are the parts of the world closest to the Equator. Many parts have two seasons, not four. In June, tropical areas north of the Equator have the strongest heat and heaviest rains. In December, it is the turn of the areas south of the Equator.

Rainy days

Rainforests have rainy weather all year round – but there is still a wet and dry season. It is just that the wet season is even wetter!

Rainforest plants get lots of water because it rains almost every day.

Wet and windy

Monsoons are winds that carry heavy rains. The rains fall in the tropics during the hot, rainy season. They can cause chaos, turning streets into rivers and even washing people's homes away.

Monsoons bring violent **thunderstorms** with heavy rain and lightning.

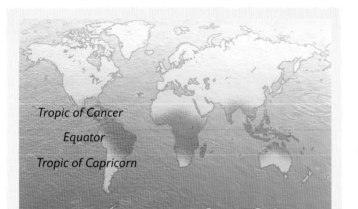

Tropic of Cancer

Equator

Tropic of Capricorn

The Tropics

The tropics (shown in orange) lie either side of the Equator, between lines of latitude called the Tropic of Cancer and the Tropic of Capricorn. The tropics are always hot, as they are constantly facing the Sun.

FUN FACT!

In parts of India, over 26,000 millimetres of rain have fallen in a single year!

Scorching Sun

The Sun is a star – a super-hot ball of burning gases. It gives off scorching-hot heat rays that travel 150 million kilometres through space to Earth.

Desert survival
In the desert, the Sun's rays scorch Earth and there is very little water. Some plants and animals have managed to find ways of surviving in these conditions.

Dust storms
Too much sun brings drought. Without rain, the dry earth turns to dust. Strong winds blow the dry earth, causing dust storms.

WILD WEATHER

Quiz time!

1 What colour are leaves in autumn?

2 What is the name of the imaginary line that runs around the middle of Earth?

3 What kind of climate will you find in the North Pole?

Q1 Picture clue

Answers 1 Golden **2** Equator **3** Cold, polar climate

The **Sahara** desert in North Africa is the sunniest place on Earth.

Camels have long eyelashes to keep sand out of their eyes.

A **mirage** is a trick of the light and makes us see things that aren't there.

Heat protection
Desert peoples cover their heads to protect them from the hot sun and sand.

The water cycle

The water cycle involves all the water
on Earth. Water vapour rises from
lakes, rivers and the sea to form
clouds in the atmosphere.

1 *Water evaporates
(disappears into the
air) from the sea*

Water, water, everywhere

Too much rain causes flooding. Flash floods
happen after a short burst of heavy rainfall.

From sea to sky
As the Sun heats the
ocean's surface, some water
turns into water vapour (a kind of
gas) and rises into the air to form clouds.
Rain falls from the clouds, some of which is
soaked up by the land, but a lot finds its
way back to the sea.

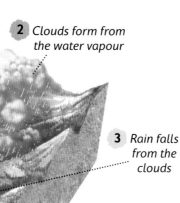

2 *Clouds form from the water vapour*

Cumulonimbus clouds give heavy rain showers.

3 *Rain falls from the clouds*

4 *Rainwater flows down mountains and into rivers*

5 *The rivers run back to the sea, and the cycle starts again*

Stratus clouds can bring drizzle or appear as fog.

Make a rain gauge

You will need
jar • marker pen • ruler • notebook • pen

1 Place the jar outside where it can collect rain.

2 Use the marker pen to mark the water level on the outside of the jar each day.

3 Keep a record of the changing levels of rainfall in a notebook.

Cirris clouds look like wisps of smoke. They are unlikely to bring rain.

Windy weather

Wind is moving air. Winds blow because air is constantly moving from areas of high pressure to areas of low pressure. The bigger the difference in temperature between the two areas, the faster the wind blows.

Beaufort Scale
Wind strength is measured on the Beaufort Scale. The scale ranges from Force 0, meaning calm, to Force 12, which is a hurricane.

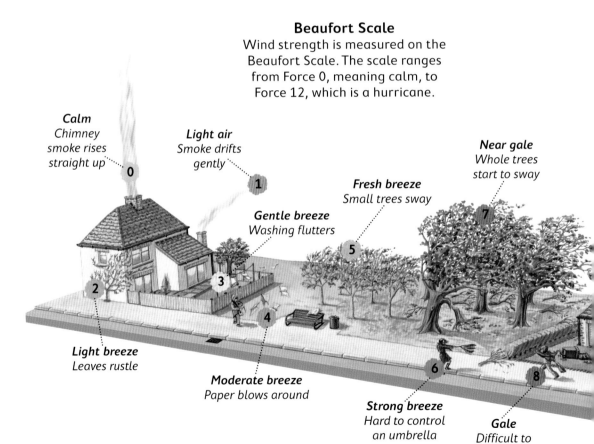

Calm
Chimney smoke rises straight up
0

Light air
Smoke drifts gently
1

Gentle breeze
Washing flutters
3

Fresh breeze
Small trees sway
5

Near gale
Whole trees start to sway
7

Light breeze
Leaves rustle
2

Moderate breeze
Paper blows around
4

Strong breeze
Hard to control an umbrella
6

Gale
Difficult to walk into wind
8

A **hurricane** is a violent tropical storm with very fast winds.

Wind power

Wind turbines can be used to make electricity. As the wind turns each turbine, the movement powers a generator and produces electricity.

The **wind** can be so strong, it blows trees over.

Severe gale
Small branches, tiles and chimneys are blown off

9

Severe storm
Serious damage

11

12

10

Storm
Houses damaged; trees blown down

Hurricane
Widespread damage

FUN FACT!

A tropical storm that starts in the Atlantic Ocean is called a hurricane. In the Pacific, it is called a typhoon. In the Indian Ocean it is a cyclone.

99

Thunder and lightning

Inside a big thundercloud, water drops and bits of ice move up and down, bumping into each other. This makes electricity build up. When the electricity jumps around, we see a spark of lightning and hear a loud clap of thunder.

Colours of lightning
Lightning comes in different colours. If there is rain in the thundercloud, the lightning looks red. If there's hail in the thundercloud, the lightning looks blue.

How close is the storm?

Thunder and lightning happen at the same time, but light travels faster than sound, so you see the lightning first.

1 When you see a lightning flash, count the seconds between the flash and the thunderclap that follows.

2 Then divide the number of seconds by three. This shows you how many kilometres away the storm is.

3 Keep a record and see if the storm comes when you think it will.

Sheet lightning travels from cloud to cloud.

Forked lightning travels from a cloud to the ground.

Hailstones
Hailstones are chunks of ice that fall from thunderclouds.

FUN FACT!
A person can survive a lightning strike. Lightning is very dangerous and can kill you, but American Roy Sullivan survived being struck seven times.

Lightning conductors
Tall buildings, such as church steeples, have lightning conductors placed on their roofs to absorb the shock.

Tornadoes and hurricanes

A tornado forms in a thunderstorm, when the back part of the thundercloud starts spinning. The spinning air forms a funnel that reaches down towards Earth. When it touches the ground, it becomes a tornado.

High speeds
A tornado spins at speeds of up to 480 kilometres an hour. It whizzes along the ground like a high-speed vacuum cleaner, sucking up everything in its path.

Hurricane Hunters

Hurricane Hunters are special weather planes that fly into the storm to take measurements. This information tells us where the hurricane will go.

Waterspouts are pillars of spinning water sucked up by a tornado.

Dust devils are desert tornadoes that create a storm of sand.

Eye of the storm
The centre of a hurricane is calm and still. This part is called the 'eye'. As the eye of the storm passes over, there is a pause in the rains and wind.

FUN FACT!
Waterspouts are so strong, they can suck up fish living in a lake!

103

Light shows

Rainbows are caused by sunlight passing through falling raindrops. The water acts like a prism (a triangle-shaped piece of glass), which splits the light.

Spot a rainbow

Rainbows are most likely to be seen towards the end of the day, especially where thunderstorms build up during hot summer days.

Remember the rainbow!

The first letter of every word of this rhyme gives the first letter of each colour of the rainbow — as it appears in the sky.		
Richard	Red
Of	Orange
York	Yellow
Gave	Green
Battle	Blue
In	Indigo
Vain	Violet

A halo looks like a circle of light around the Sun.

Curtains of light

In the far north and far south of the world, amazing patterns of light sometimes appear in the sky. These colourful curtains are called auroras. They occur when tiny particles of light from the Sun smash into the air.

Mock suns are two bright spots that appear on either side of the Sun.

Quiz time!

1 What are weather maps called?

2 Where do monsoons occur?

3 When is it summer in the Northern Hemisphere?

4 What are dust devils?

Q1 Picture clue

Fogbows happen when sunlight passes through fog.

3 June to September 4 Desert tornadoes

Answers 1 Synoptic charts **2** In the tropics

105

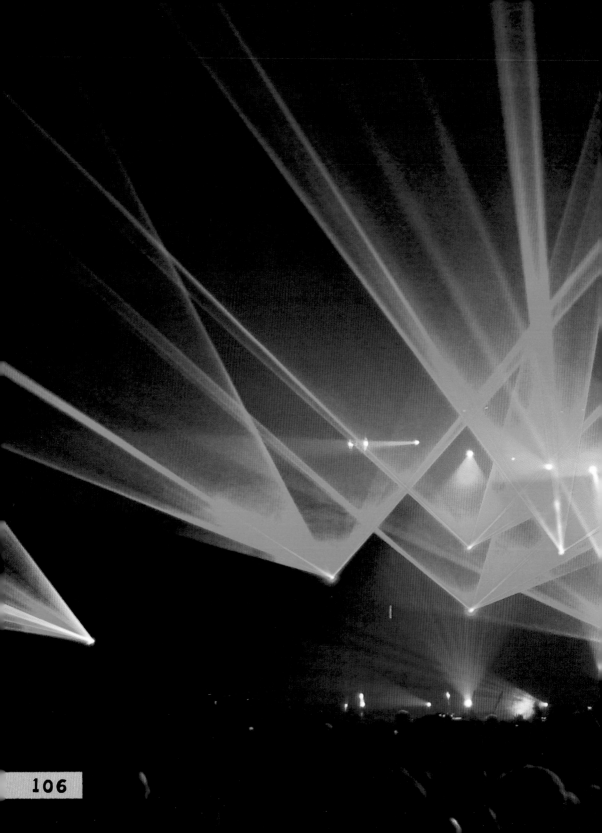

SUPER SCIENCE

Our world of science

Science is all around us. Toasters, bicycles, mobile phones, cars, computers, light bulbs — all the gadgets and machines we use every day are the result of scientific discoveries.

Feeling forces

Pushes and pulls make things stop and start. Scientists use the word 'force' for pushes and pulls. Forces are all around us. The force of gravity pulls things downwards. It makes a rollercoaster car hurtle downhill.

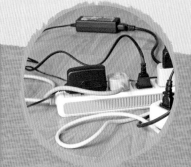

Electricity is a type of energy that makes lots of things around us work.

Hidden strength

Skyscrapers stay up because they have a strong frame on the inside. The frame is made from steel and concrete. These are very strong materials. The frame is hidden by the skyscraper's walls.

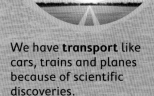

We have **transport** like cars, trains and planes because of scientific discoveries.

Space exploration is a type of science.

Machines are everywhere

Machines help us to do many things, or they make doing them easier. Machines are all around you – from a see-saw in the park to the wheel on a car.

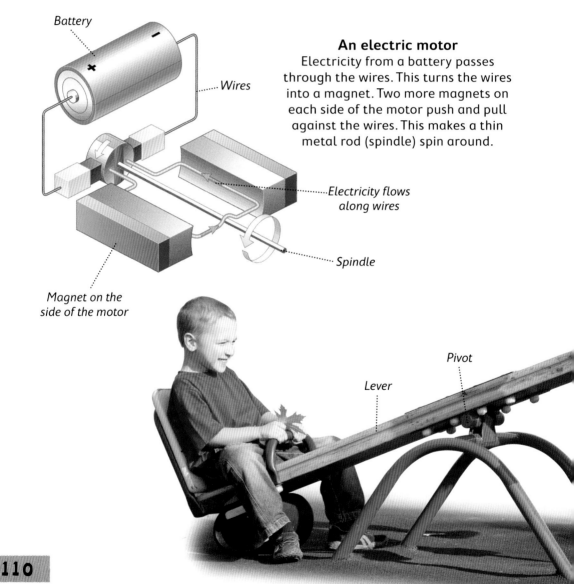

Battery

Wires

An electric motor
Electricity from a battery passes through the wires. This turns the wires into a magnet. Two more magnets on each side of the motor push and pull against the wires. This makes a thin metal rod (spindle) spin around.

Electricity flows along wires

Spindle

Magnet on the side of the motor

Pivot

Lever

110

Inside a wheel

A wheel is a very simple machine that can spin around. Wheels let other machines, such as skateboards, bicycles, cars and trains, roll along smoothly. They also make it easy to move heavy weights in carts and wheelbarrows.

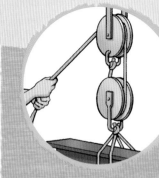

A **pulley** is a simple machine that is used for lifting heavy weights.

A **screw** changes a small turning motion into a powerful motion.

FUN FACT!

A ramp is a simple machine called an inclined plane. It is easier to walk up a ramp than to jump straight to the top.

Using a lever

A see-saw is a simple machine called a lever. It has a long arm and a point in the middle called a pivot. As you ride on the see-saw, the lever tips up and down on the pivot.

Hot science

Heat is important in many ways. We cook with heat, warm our homes and heat water. Even factories use heat to make products, such as plastic toys.

Fizz! Crackle! Bang!
Fireworks flash and bang because they are full of chemicals that burn. The chemicals have lots of energy stored in them. When they burn, the energy changes to light, heat and sound.

How candles burn
When the candle wick is lit, the wax around it melts. The wick soaks up the liquid wax and the heat of the flame turns the wax into a gas (vapour), which burns away. As the wax becomes vapour it cools the wick, allowing the candle to burn slowly.

Hot air rises from a candle. This movement of heat is called **convection**.

A hot drink passes its heat to the spoon, warming it up. Heat moves by **conduction**.

Carrying heat

You will need
wooden ruler • metal spoon • plastic spatula
heatproof jug • frozen peas • butter

1 Fix a frozen pea with butter to the end of the ruler, spoon and spatula.

2 Put the other ends in a heatproof jug. Ask an adult to fill the jug with hot water.

3 Heat is conducted (passed on) from the water, up the object, to melt the butter. Which object is the best conductor?

A thermometer is used for measuring heat.

113

Light at work

Light is energy that you can see. Light waves are tiny. About 2000 of them laid end to end would stretch across this full stop.

Splitting light
Light rays travel in straight lines. When light shines through a prism, the rays bend. When sunlight (white light) passes through a prism it splits into many colours, like a rainbow.

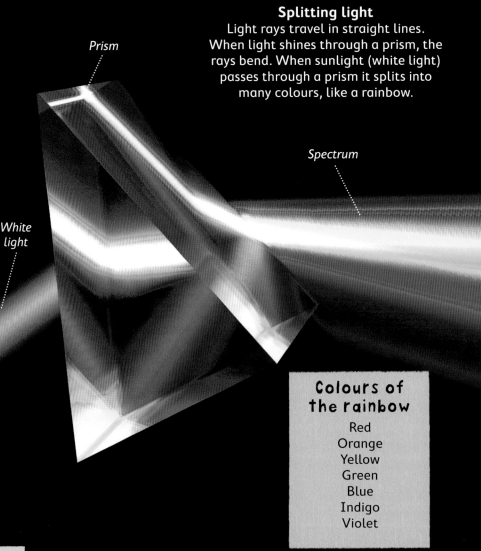

Prism

Spectrum

White light

Colours of the rainbow
Red
Orange
Yellow
Green
Blue
Indigo
Violet

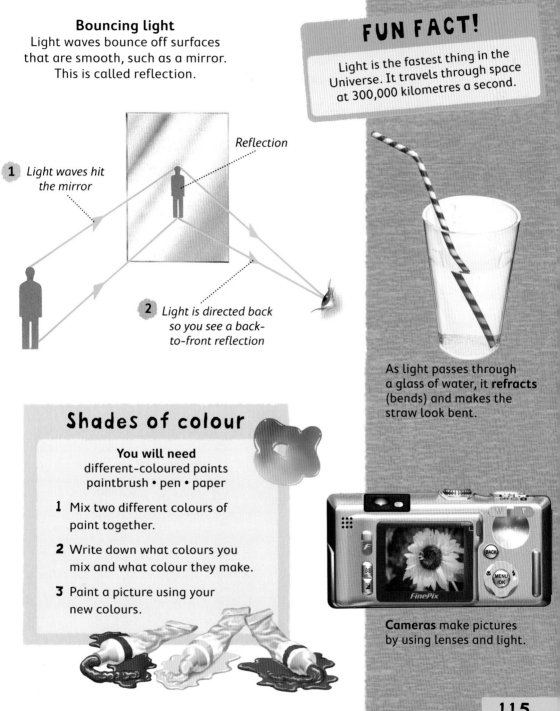

Bouncing light
Light waves bounce off surfaces that are smooth, such as a mirror. This is called reflection.

Reflection

1 *Light waves hit the mirror*

2 *Light is directed back so you see a back-to-front reflection*

FUN FACT!
Light is the fastest thing in the Universe. It travels through space at 300,000 kilometres a second.

As light passes through a glass of water, it **refracts** (bends) and makes the straw look bent.

Shades of colour

You will need
different-coloured paints
paintbrush • pen • paper

1 Mix two different colours of paint together.

2 Write down what colours you mix and what colour they make.

3 Paint a picture using your new colours.

Cameras make pictures by using lenses and light.

What a noise!

Listening to the radio or television depend on the science of sound. Sounds are carried by invisible waves in the air, which travel about 330 metres a second. This is one million times slower than light waves.

The decibel scale
Scientists measure the loudness of sound in decibels (dB). One of the loudest sounds that we hear is a jet plane engine.

Thunder 100 db

Atom bomb 210 db
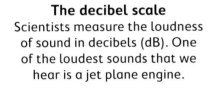

Talking 40 db

Jet taking off 140 db

Rustling leaves 10db

Making the journey

We cannot see sound waves but we can hear them using our ears. Sound waves travel through the ear to our brain.

4 *Sound waves vibrate through the fluid in the cochlea and travel to the brain*

3 *Tiny bones carry vibrations*

2 *Eardrum vibrates*

1 *Noise travels to the ear*

FUN FACT!

Sounds waves bounce off hard, flat surfaces. This is called an echo.

Loudspeakers change electrical signals into sound waves.

Box guitar

You will need
shoebox • elastic band • split pins • card

1 Cut a hole about 10 centimetres across on one side of an empty shoebox.

2 Push split pins through either side of the hole, and stretch an elastic band between them.

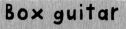

3 Pluck the band. Hear how the air vibrates inside the box — like a guitar.

When you speak, **sound waves** spread out so everyone can hear what you say.

Magnet power

Magnetism is an invisible force that pulls things together or pushes them apart. Magnets are made from lumps of iron or steel. You can turn a piece of iron into a magnet by stroking it with another magnet.

Magnetic machine
A magnet can also be made by sending electricity through a coil of wire. This is called an electromagnet. Some electromagnets are so strong, they can pick up cars.

A magnet has two different **poles** – north and south.

Floating train
Maglev (magnetic levitation) trains float above the track. Magnets underneath the train and in the track repel (push) each other.

Electromagnets are so strong they can lift whole cars.

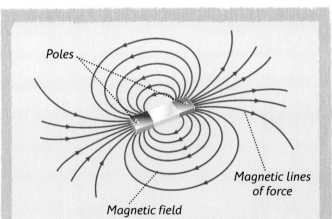

Poles

Magnetic lines of force

Magnetic field

The force of a magnet
A magnet is a block of iron or steel. A force surrounds the magnet, in a region called the magnetic field. The magnetic field is strongest at the two parts of the magnet called the poles.

A car's body is made from **iron-based steel**, which is magnetic.

119

What is electricity?

Electricity is energy that flows from a power station to our homes. It is used all around us to power washing machines, vacuum cleaners and kettles. Electricity is made by the movement of electrons inside atoms.

Hopping electrons
When electrons are 'pushed', they hop from one atom to the next. This is how electricity flows.

Electron

Atom

Checking cables
Electricity from power stations is carried along cables on high pylons. It is very powerful, and so extremely dangerous. When cables need to be checked, the electricity is turned off well in advance.

Where it comes from

A power station makes enough electricity for thousands of homes.

Generator

Cables

Pylon

Solar panels can make electricity from the Sun's light energy.

A **battery** makes electricity from different chemicals, such as an acid and a metal, swapping electrons.

Make a circuit

You will need
lightbulb • battery • wire

1 Ask an adult to help. Join a bulb to a battery with pieces of wire, as shown.

2 Electricity flows from the battery, through the wires to the lightbulb, in a circuit (loop) and lights the bulb.

Pylons hold cables safely above the ground.

Making sounds and pictures

The air is full of waves we cannot see or hear, unless we have the right machine. Radio waves are a form of electrical and magnetic energy, just like light waves and microwaves. They all travel at an equal speed — the speed of light.

A radio picks up radio waves using its long aerial or antenna and converts them to sound waves

Sometimes radio waves may be sent by a satellite in space

Radio waves

Travelling waves
Radio waves are used for both radio and television. They travel long distances from a satellite to your home, car or workplace.

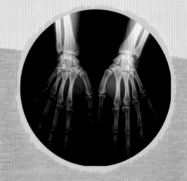

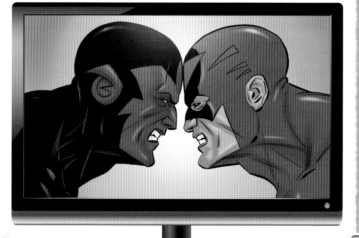

X-rays can go through the soft parts of your body and take pictures of the bones.

Receiving waves
A radio receiver converts radio waves into sounds. A television receiver or TV set changes them to pictures and sounds.

Microwaves are a kind of radio wave. They are used to cook food.

FUN FACT!

Radio waves travel easily though space, but they hardly pass at all through water.

A satellite dish on the outside of a house picks up radio waves for TV channels

Laser power

Laser light is a special kind of light. It is just
one pure colour, where as ordinary white light
is a mixture of colours. Laser light can travel
long distances as a strong, straight beam.

Bright lights
At a concert or a light
show, different coloured
laser beams sweep to and
fro. They pierce the
darkness, making a
spectacular sight.

Everyday lasers

Lasers have lots of everyday uses. They are used to play CDs and DVDs, and in computers.

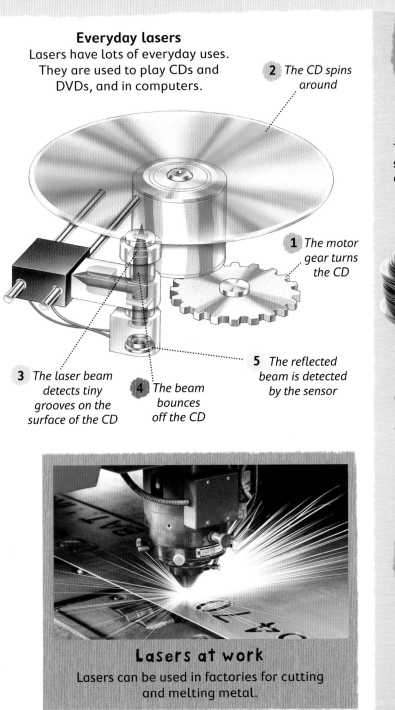

2 *The CD spins around*

1 *The motor gear turns the CD*

3 *The laser beam detects tiny grooves on the surface of the CD*

4 *The beam bounces off the CD*

5 *The reflected beam is detected by the sensor*

The beam from a **laser spirit level** gives accurate measurements.

CDs and DVDs can be used to store music, films and information.

Lasers at work

Lasers can be used in factories for cutting and melting metal.

Special **cables** called fibre optics use lasers to carry phone calls and television programmes.

Computer science

Computers are amazing machines. We give them
instructions and information, in various ways.
These include typing on a keyboard, inserting
a disc, using a joystick, or linking up a camera,
scanner or another computer.

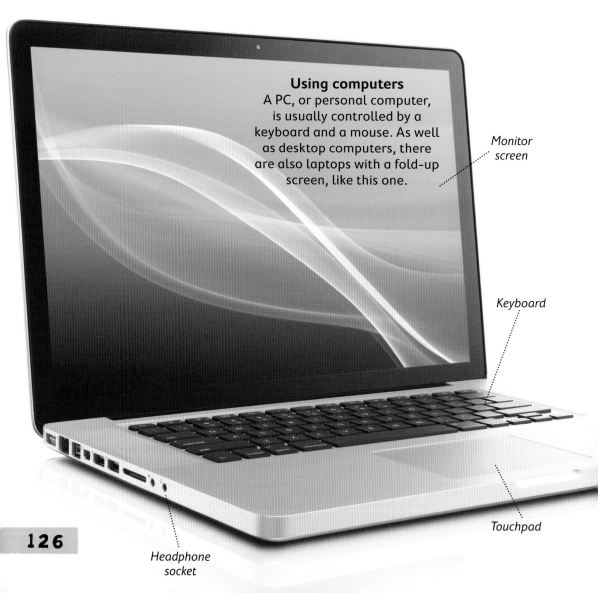

Using computers
A PC, or personal computer,
is usually controlled by a
keyboard and a mouse. As well
as desktop computers, there
are also laptops with a fold-up
screen, like this one.

Monitor screen

Keyboard

Touchpad

Headphone socket

Microchips are the main 'brain' of a computer.

On a tablet
The iPad was first introduced by Apple™ in 2010. It is a 'tablet', which works like a computer but is much thinner and lighter.

The **mouse** moves a pointer around the computer screen.

Quiz time!

1 What does PC stand for?

2 What speed do radio waves travel at?

3 What do most magnetic substances contain?

4 What do you call the main brain of a computer?

Q2 Picture clue

Answers 1 Personal computer
2 Speed of light 3 Iron 4 Microchips

Information can be stored on a chip inside a **memory stick**.

Amazing web

The world is at your fingertips — if you are on the Internet. The Internet is one of the most amazing results of modern-day science. It is a worldwide network of computers, linked like one huge electrical spider's web.

Inventing the Internet

The Internet as we know it today was invented in 1989. Tim Berners-Lee and his team wanted to make information easier for people to find.

Internet on the go

Many mobile phones are able to access the Internet. You can browse websites, send emails and watch videos.

A website is like an electronic version of a leaflet or book.

Lots to say

There are many different websites. Some of the most popular include 'social networking' sites where friends can talk to each other and share photographs. To look up information, we use search engines or browsers, such as Google and Yahoo. People can share videos on Youtube.

Telephone wires carry signals from one place to another.

Quiz time!

1 What measures heat?

2 How many dB does a jet plane produce?

3 What is the science of sound called?

4 What is the centre of an atom called?

Q1 Picture clue

Answers 1 Thermometer **2** 140 dB **3** Acoustics **4** Nucleus

Email means electronic mail – sending messages over the Internet.

What is it made of?

You would not make a bridge out of straw,
or a cup out of thin paper. Choosing the right
material is important. Cars are made from tough,
long-lasting materials. Metal, plastic and rubber
are all materials used to make cars.

The right substances
A racing car has thousands of parts
made from hundreds of materials.
Many parts need to be strong, but
not weigh much, so the car can go
as fast as possible.

*The engine is very powerful,
but also needs to be light*

*The main body of the car is
made from carbon fibre. It is
strong and light, and protects
the car from damage*

Plastics are mainly made from oil.

Not built to last

In 2007, this bridge in Minneapolis, USA, collapsed. The road and the vehicles that travelled on it were too heavy.

Ceramics are made from clay that is dug from the earth.

Made by nature

Many materials come from plants. Wood comes from the trunks and branches of trees. Cotton comes from the seeds of cotton plants to make clothes such as T-shirts.

Glass is made from limestone and sand.

Mini science

Everything in the world is made of atoms. Atoms are the smallest bits of a substance. They are so tiny that even a billion atoms would be too small to see.

Looking inside
Inside an atom are even smaller bits called subatomic particles. There are three main kinds – protons, neutrons and electrons.

Inside an atom

1 The centre of the atom is called the nucleus. It contains protons, neutrons and electrons

2 Protons

3 Neutrons

4 Electrons

5 The movement of electrons around the nucleus

Proton

Electron

Hydrogen is a gas with just one proton.

Proton

Neutron

Helium is a gas with two protons and two neutrons.

Proton

Neutron

Oxygen, the gas we need to breathe, has eight protons and eight neutrons.

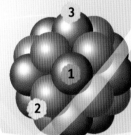

3

1

2

4   5

FUN FACT!

Atoms are so small that a grain of sand contains at least 100 billion billion atoms!

133

Science and nature

Scientists study animals, plants, rocks and soil. They want to understand nature and find out how science and its technology affect wildlife. Ecologists study how animals and plants live and grow.

Solving problems

Scientists study the damage and pollution power stations, factories and heavy traffic have on the environment. They then try to solve these problems.

Key

1	Heron	4	Power station
2	Otter	5	Reedmace
3	Warbler		

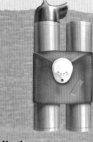

Radio beacons can be used to track animals in the wild.

Ecology in danger

Oil spills and leaks cause great damage to an area's wildlife. Scientists find the best ways to clear up the pollution.

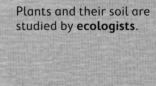

Plants and their soil are studied by **ecologists**.

Keeping track

Ecologists use radio-collars to track endangered tigers, so they can understand the threats facing them, and how to save them.

FUN FACT!

Science explains how birds find their way across the world. They use the Earth's magnetism, so they know which way is north or south.

Healthy Science

Medical scientists work to produce better drugs,
more spare parts for the body and more
machines for hospitals. They also
carry out scientific research to
find out how people can stay
healthy and prevent disease.

Medical machine
An ECG machine shows the heart beating.
Sensor pads are stuck to the body. Then
the machine picks up tiny pulses of
electricity from your muscles and nerves.
The pulses are then displayed as a wavy
line on the screen.

Make a pulse machine

You will need
modelling clay • a drinking straw

1 Find your pulse by feeling your wrist.

2 Place some modelling clay on this area, and stick a drinking straw into it. Watch the straw twitch with each heartbeat.

3 Now you can see and feel your pulse. Check your pulse rate by counting the number of heartbeats in one minute.

A **thermometer** is used to check body temperature.

The right tools
Laser beams are ideal for delicate operations, such as eye surgery. The beam is very powerful and precise.

A **blood pressure monitor** can tell doctors if a person's blood pressure is too high or too low.

Laser beam is shone into the eye

Laser beam hits retina inside the eye

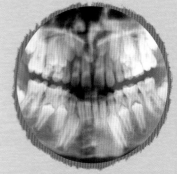

X-rays are used to take photographs of bones and teeth.

137

DEADLY DINOSAURS

What are dinosaurs?

Dinosaurs were reptiles – a group of animals with scaly skin that lived millions of years ago. There were many different kinds of dinosaur, but they all died out long, long ago.

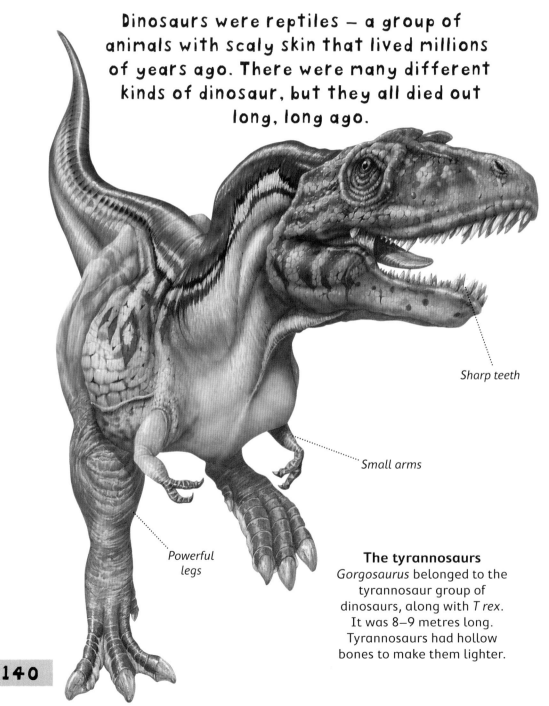

Sharp teeth

Small arms

Powerful legs

The tyrannosaurs
Gorgosaurus belonged to the tyrannosaur group of dinosaurs, along with *T rex*. It was 8–9 metres long. Tyrannosaurs had hollow bones to make them lighter.

140

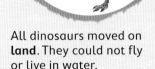

Before *T rex*

Guanlong is known as 'crown dragon' because it had horn-like plate of bone on its nose. It was around nearly 100 million years before *Tyrannosaurus rex*.

All dinosaurs moved on **land**. They could not fly or live in water.

We can learn about dinosaurs through their remains, or **fossils**.

Famous dinosaur

Tyrannosaurus rex is the most well-known fearsome dinosaur. When eating large prey, it would tear the flesh, gulp it in lumps and swallow it whole.

Some **dinosaurs** were plant eaters, while others ate meat.

When were they around?

Dinosaurs lived between 230 million and 65 million years ago. This vast length of time is called the Mesozoic Era, or the Age of Dinosaurs. The Mesozoic Era was split into three time periods — the Triassic, Jurassic and Cretaceous.

Triassic Period 251–200 million years ago

The dinosaurs first appeared in the Triassic Period. Fossils of the earliest dinosaurs are from the mid-Triassic Period, about 230 million years ago. Around the end of the Triassic Period, the dinosaurs became much stronger, as they could stand upright, on two feet.

Standing on **two feet** meant the dinosaurs could run faster and further.

Jurassic Period 200–145 million years ago

During the Jurassic Period, dinosaurs reached their greatest size and spread around the world. The biggest dinosaurs were the sauropods, or 'lizard feet'. Long-necked herbivores were hunted by powerful carnivores.

When the dinosaurs died out, **mammals** became the main land animals.

Cretaceous Period 145–65 million years ago

Many different types of dinosaur developed during the Cretaceous Period. Thousands of fossils from this period have been discovered, such as the small but deadly carnivore, *Deinonychus*.

FUN FACT!

The word dinosaur means 'terrible lizard'. However, dinosaurs weren't really lizards, and not all of them were terrible!

143

Life before dinosaurs

Dinosaurs were not the first animals on Earth. Many other creatures lived before them, including other types of reptiles. Over millions of years, one of these groups of reptiles changed very slowly, or evolved, into the first dinosaurs.

Reptile relation
Dimetrodon was a fierce reptile that looked like a dinosaur – but it wasn't. It lived 270 million years ago, before the time of the dinosaurs.

Land crocodiles
Protosuchus was an early type of crocodile. It lived in North America about 190 million years ago. Unlike modern crocodiles, it lived and hunted on land.

Super swimmer

Some reptiles, such as *Mosasaurus*, lived in the sea, and were as big and fierce as dinosaurs. *Mosasaurus* had razor-sharp teeth and could swim at speed to catch its prey.

Chasmatosaurus had teeth on the roof of its mouth as well as in its jaws.

Cynognathus was a type of reptile, but had fur instead of scaly skin.

Moschops was a plant-eating reptile with very long, sharp teeth.

Quiz time!

1 What type of animal was a dinosaur?

2 What is the name of the era in which dinosaurs lived?

3 What is a carnivore?

4 Which period is missing – Triassic, Cretaceous and –?

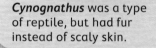

Q4 Picture clue

Answers 1 Reptile 2 Mesozoic Era 3 Meat eater 4 Jurassic

Early dinosaurs

The earliest dinosaurs walked the Earth almost 230 million years ago. They lived in what is now Argentina, in South America. They included Herrerasaurus.

Sharp teeth in long jaws

On two legs
Herrerasaurus was a meat-eating dinosaur. It could stand almost upright and run on its two rear legs, making it one of the fastest dinosaurs of its time.

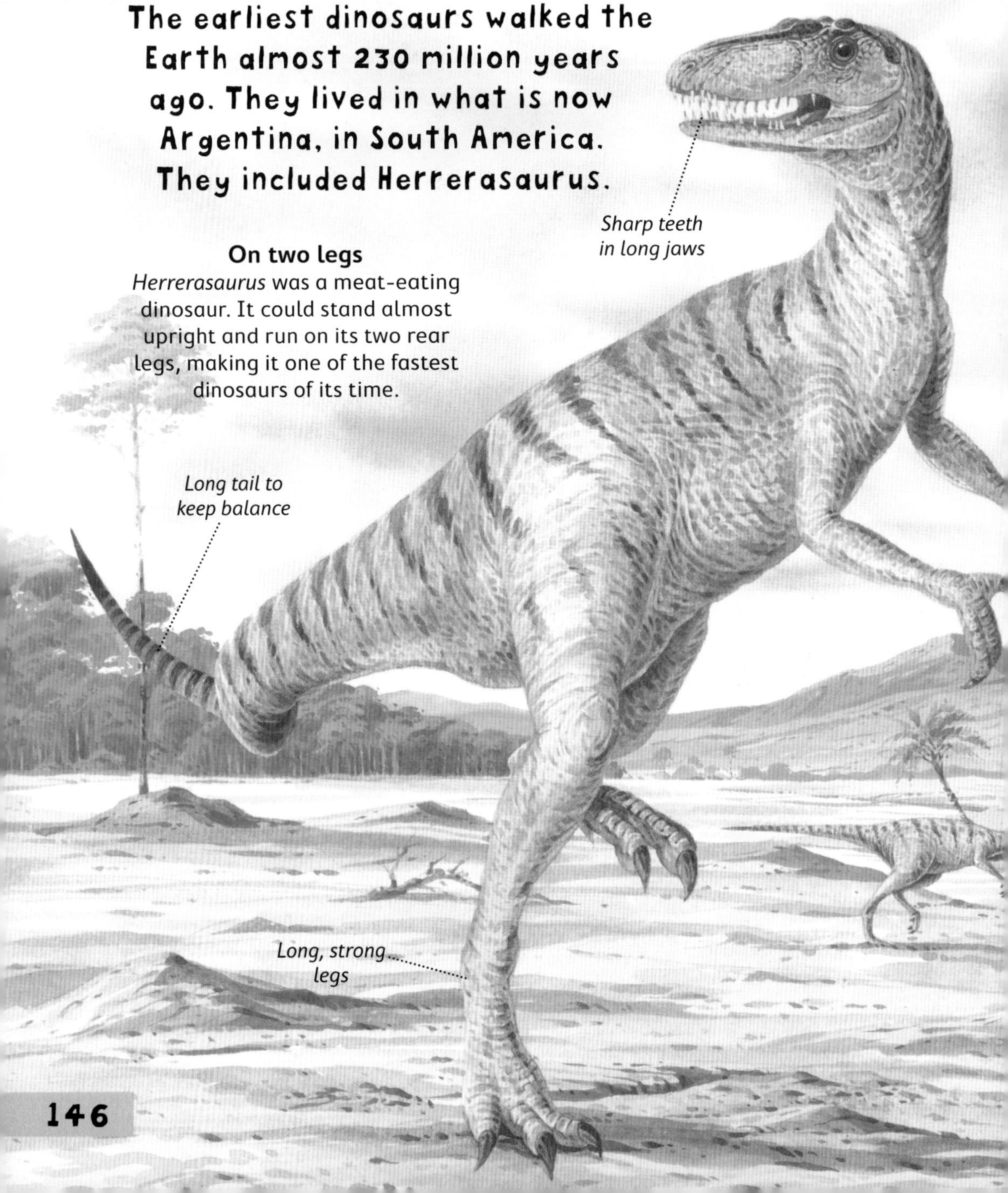

Long tail to keep balance

Long, strong legs

Make a dinosaur

You will need
pencil • paints • stiff card • scissors
sticky tape • split pins

1 Draw a dinosaur without legs. Paint it any colour you wish and cut it out.

2 Draw two legs on another piece of card. Paint and cut them out, too.

3 Fix the legs on either side of the hip area of the body using a split pin. Now make your dinosaur move!

Long head and bendy neck

Hands with no claws

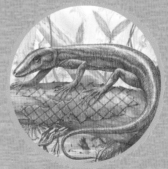

Herrerasaurus had legs underneath its body, not out to the side like other animals.

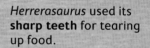

Herrerasaurus used its **sharp teeth** for tearing up food.

Early meat-eating dinosaurs **hunted small animals** such as lizards.

Changing dinosaurs

As the early dinosaurs spread over the land,
they began to change. This natural change in
living things has happened since life began on
Earth. New kinds of plants and animals appear,
live for a time, and then die out as more
new kinds appear. This is called evolution.

Herbivore or carnivore?
Some dinosaurs, such as *Massospondylus*,
grew larger and began to eat plants
rather than animals. The fossils of
dinosaur teeth show which food
each type of dinosaur ate.

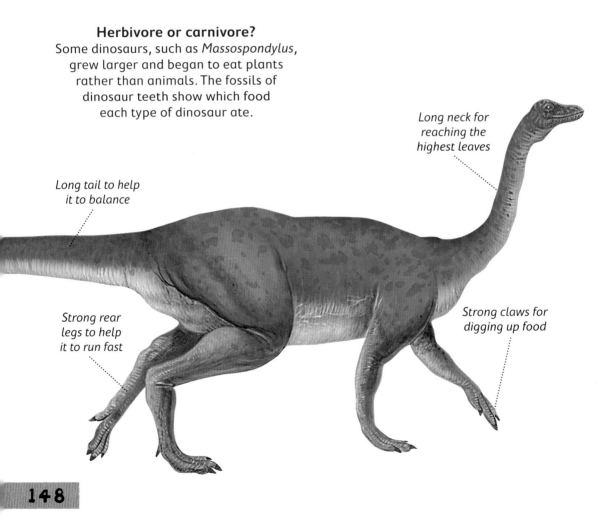

Long neck for
reaching the
highest leaves

Long tail to help
it to balance

Strong rear
legs to help
it to run fast

Strong claws for
digging up food

Stronger and safer

Early plant-eating dinosaurs may have become larger so that they could reach up into the trees for food. Being bigger meant they were also safer from enemies.

Plateosaurus had thumbs that ended in a large spike, for jabbing at enemies.

Plateosaurus *was one of the first big plant-eating dinosaurs*

Riojasaurus *weighed about one tonne – as much as a family car*

Riojasaurus probably moved on all fours, but reared up on its back legs to reach leaves.

FUN FACT!

Early plant-eating dinosaurs did not eat fruits or grasses – these hadn't appeared yet! Instead they ate plants such as horsetails and ferns.

Rutiodon *was a crocodile-like meat eater. It hunted dinosaurs such as* Plateosaurus *and* Riojasaurus

Gentle giants

Sauropods were dinosaur giants. These enormous creatures all had small heads, long necks, long tails, barrel-shaped bodies and four legs.

Towering above

Barosaurus was one of the biggest sauropods at about 25 metres long. Like most sauropods, *Barosaurus* had to eat for most of the day to get enough goodness for its enormous body.

150

Size and scale

Some of the biggest sauropods were *Brachiosaurus*, *Argentinosaurus* and *Apatosaurus*. This scale shows how big they were compared to an adult human.

Apatosaurus *was 23 metres long. Its tail had 82 bones and was used to whip enemies*

Brachiosaurus *was 25 metres long. With its long front legs and neck, it could reach food 14 metres from the ground*

Diplodocus had peglike teeth for raking up leaves.

Colossal creature

Argentinosaurus was the biggest sauropod at 40 metres in length and 100 tonnes in weight.

Sauropods had claws that were almost flat. Some even looked like they had toenails!

Huge hunters

The biggest meat-eating dinosaurs were the largest hunters ever to have lived. Different types came and went during the Age of Dinosaurs. One of the last dinosaurs was also one of the largest hunters — Tyrannosaurus rex.

Massive head measuring 1.6 metres in length

Small, useless arms

Bone-cruncher
Tyrannosaurus rex had sharp teeth up to 25 centimetres in length. Its jaws could crunch through bone.

Huge feet and powerful legs

152

Built for hunting

Predators like *Tyrannosaurus rex* had strong legs for running, and enormous toe claws for kicking and holding down victims.

Giganotosaurus is the biggest meat-eating animal that has ever lived.

Powerful predator

Allosaurus was a big, fast-moving hunter with powerful jaws. It lived millions of years before *Tyrannosaurus rex*.

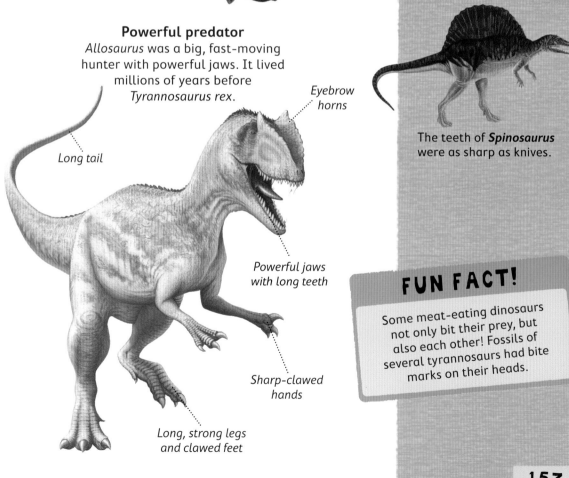

The teeth of **Spinosaurus** were as sharp as knives.

Long tail

Eyebrow horns

Powerful jaws with long teeth

Sharp-clawed hands

Long, strong legs and clawed feet

FUN FACT!

Some meat-eating dinosaurs not only bit their prey, but also each other! Fossils of several tyrannosaurs had bite marks on their heads.

Super senses

Like the reptiles of today, dinosaurs could see, hear and smell the world around them. We know this from the fossils of dead dinosaurs. Fossil skulls have spaces for eyes, ears and nostrils.

Seeing in the dark

Troodon had very big eyes, which may have helped it to see in the dark when chasing prey, such as lizards, birds and small mammals.

Long, whip-like tail

Narrow jaws

Strong senses
Fossils of *Troodon* have shown that it had a large brain, and good senses of sight, hearing and smell.

Feathered arms

Long, curved claw on foot

Slim legs

154

Make a Troodon mask

You will need
card • paints • scissors • elastic band

1 Draw and paint the mask shown here.

2 Carefully cut out the mask and give it two large eye holes.

3 Make a small hole on either side of the mask to thread cotton through, so you can tie the mask onto your head and become a *Troodon* dinosaur!

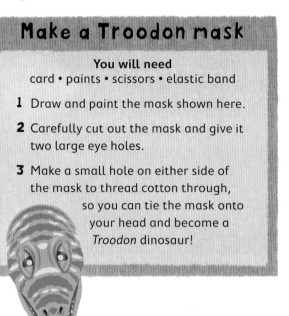

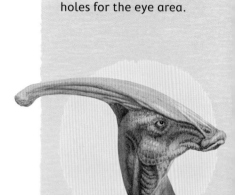

Troodon's skull had large holes for the eye area.

Parasaurolophus may have used the tube-like crest on its head to make a noise like a trumpet.

Brainbox

Tyrannosaurus rex had the biggest brain of almost any dinosaur. Some fossils show the space where its brain would have been, and its shape.

Brain

Corythosaurus had a bony plate on its head, instead of a tube.

Slow or speedy?

Dinosaurs moved at different speeds, depending on their size and shape. Today, fast-moving cheetahs and ostriches are slim animals with long legs. Elephants and hippos are heavy and move slowly. Dinosaurs were similar — some were fast and some were slow.

Fast features
Ornithomimus had long, strong legs. It was able to run fast to escape from predators. *Ornithomimus* could reach a speed of 70 kilometres an hour. That's faster than a horse at full gallop!

156

Feeding time

Ornithomimus' mouth was shaped like a bird's beak. It pecked at all kinds of food such as seeds, worms and bugs. Its head was too small to be able to hunt large prey.

Struthiomimus could run at 80 kilometres an hour.

Coelophysis could run quickly after its prey of lizards and insects.

Muttaburrasaurus could only run at 15 kilometres an hour.

Quiz time!

1 What was the biggest sauropod?

2 How long were *Tyrannosaurus'* teeth?

3 Which dinosaur had huge eyes?

4 How fast could *Ornithomimus* run?

Q2 Picture clue

Answers 1 *Argentinosaurus* **2** 25 centimetres **3** *Troodon* **4** 70 kilometres an hour

Eggs and nests

Like most reptiles today, dinosaurs produced young by laying eggs. These hatched out into baby dinosaurs that gradually grew into adults. Fossils have been found of eggs with dinosaurs still developing inside, as well as fossils of newly hatched baby dinosaurs.

Laying eggs
Protoceratops laid its eggs in circles inside a bowl-shaped nest in the ground. The mother protected its eggs from hungry hunters.

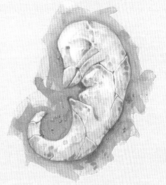

Tyrannosaurus rex's **sausage-shaped eggs** were 40 centimetres long and 15 centimetres wide.

A **fossilized embryo** developing inside an egg.

Inside the egg

A baby dinosaur developed as an embryo in its egg. It was fed by nutrients from the yolk.

Yolk

Embryo

Some dinosaur eggs were **leathery and bendy**, like reptile eggs today.

Baby dinosaurs

Some dinosaurs may have looked after their babies, and brought them food in the nest. Fossils of Maiasaura that have been found include nests, eggs, newly hatched young and broken eggshells.

Baby Maiasaura *were only 30 to 40 centimetres long*

Design a dinosaur

You will need
paper • paints

1 Draw your own dinosaur — you could add horns, sharp teeth, sharp claws, a long tail, big eyes — anything you want!

2 No one knows what colour dinosaurs actually were, so you could paint your dinosaur any colour — purple and green with red spikes!

3 Name your dinosaur. You could name it after yourself, like *Clarosaurus* or *Pauloceratops*!

Some dinosaurs laid **eggs** that were 50 times as big as a hen's egg.

Some babies hatched by **biting** through the tough shell.

Hungry babies
Newly hatched *Maiasaura* babies stayed in their nest until their legs were strong enough for them to move around. The parents brought food, such as berries, to the nest for the babies to eat.

The nest was a mound of mud about 2 metres across and contained about 20 eggs

FUN FACT!
Baby dinosaurs grew up to five times faster than human babies. Some were already one metre long when they hatched!

Dinosaurs in battle

Some dinosaurs had body defences, such as spikes, to protect them from predators. Most armoured dinosaurs were plant eaters. They had to defend themselves against meat eaters such as Tyrannosaurus rex.

Spinosaurus *was a deadly carnivore with large, sharp teeth* ·········

Armour and weapons

Ankylosaurus could defend itself well. It had a large tail club to hit predators and its head and back were protected by large bony lumps and plates.

Quiz time!

1 How long were baby *Maiasaura*?

2 Was *Dimetrodon* a dinosaur?

3 What is the biggest meat-eating animal ever to have lived?

Q3 Picture clue

Answers **1** 30 to 40 centimetres **2** No, a reptile **3** *Gigantosaurus*

Triceratops had three horns, one on its nose and two above its eyes.

Ankylosaurus' *tail club was one metre across and could deliver a painful blow*

Kentrosaurus had a double row of long, bony plates and spikes.

Ankylosaurus *had spikes and lumps of bone on its back to protect itself*

Euoplocephalus had pointed lumps of bone across its back.

Where did they go?

The dinosaurs died out 65 million years ago. There are dinosaur fossils in rocks up to this time, but none after this. However, there are fossils of creatures such as fish and mammals. Perhaps a giant rock (meteorite) from space smashed into Earth, killing the dinosaurs.

Deadly meteorite
A meteorite would have thrown up clouds of ash and dust, blocking out the Sun. Plants would have died, leaving no food for the plant-eating dinosaurs. When the plant eaters died, the meat-eating dinosaurs would have starved.

Erupting volcanoes

Volcanoes around Earth could have erupted at the same time. This would have thrown out red-hot rocks, ash, dust and clouds of poison gas. Dinosaurs would have choked and died in the gloom.

Other animals may have eaten all the dinosaur eggs.

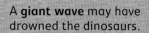

A **giant wave** may have drowned the dinosaurs.

Finding fossils

We know about dinosaurs, including how they looked and what they ate, because scientists have found and studied fossils.

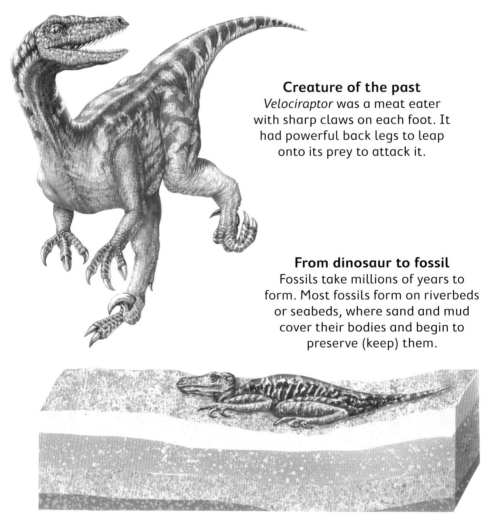

Creature of the past
Velociraptor was a meat eater with sharp claws on each foot. It had powerful back legs to leap onto its prey to attack it.

From dinosaur to fossil
Fossils take millions of years to form. Most fossils form on riverbeds or seabeds, where sand and mud cover their bodies and begin to preserve (keep) them.

 A dinosaur dies and falls into a river or lake. The soft body parts rot away, or are eaten by other animals.

By finding fossils, scientists can rebuild **dinosaur skeletons**.

2 *The bones and teeth are buried under layers of mud. Tiny pieces of rock slowly 'soak' into the bones, filling any gaps.*

A fossil of one of the smallest dinosaurs, ***Compsognathus***, was found in Germany.

3 *Over millions of year, these tiny pieces of rock replace the bones, but keep their shape. The bones have become fossils.*

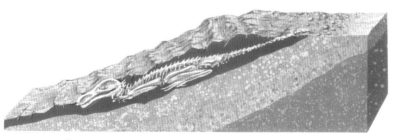

4 *If the rock containing the fossils is revealed, perhaps by wind or weather, scientists may find the fossils.*

Dinosaur skin can sometimes form fossils and show how scaly it was.

The big dig

Every year, thousands of dinosaur fossils are discovered. From the fossils, scientists try to work out what the dinosaur looked like and how it lived millions of years ago. Scientists who study prehistoric life are called palaeontologists.

Finding fossils

Most dinosaur fossils are found by hard work. Palaeontologists choose an area where fossils are most likely to be. They spend weeks chipping and digging the rock. They look closely at every tiny piece to see if it is part of a fossil.

Key

1 Scientists dig into the rock with hammers and brushes

2 Notes and sketches are records of what has been found

3 Fossils are carefully lifted to stop them cracking

Quiz time!

1 What big lump of rock from space could have destroyed the dinosaurs?

2 How long ago did the dinosaurs die out?

3 Where do most fossils form — on the land or in rivers and seas?

Q3 Picture clue

Fossilized **dinosaur tracks** have been uncovered in Colorado, USA.

Answers **1** Meteorite **2** 65 million years ago **3** Rivers and seas

What a discovery!
Some dinosaur fossils are found by luck. People out walking in the countryside come across a fossil tooth or bone by chance.

Scientists work out where each part belongs and put them back together.

3

Rebuilt skeletons are often displayed in **museums**.

OCEAN LIFE

Sea mammals

Many animals that live in the sea, such as whales and dolphins, are warm-blooded mammals. They need to come to the surface to breathe air. Dolphins can only hold their breath for a few minutes, but sperm whales can hold their breath for up to two hours.

Working together
Bottlenose dolphins swim together around a group of fish. By working as a team, they can catch more fish to eat.

Keeping warm
The polar bear lives at the North Pole. It is a good swimmer. Thick fur and a layer of fat under its skin keep the polar bear warm in the icy sea.

Most **seals** live in cold waters in the Arctic and Antarctic.

Dugongs feed on sea grass and algae on the seabed.

FUN FACT!

Barnacles are shellfish. They attach themselves to ships' hulls, or the bodies of grey whales and other large sea animals.

Cold-blooded creatures

Cold-blooded creatures, such as reptiles, cannot control their body temperature. Most of them prefer to live on land, where it is easier for them to warm up. Some reptiles have adapted to ocean life, such as marine iguanas.

Sunbathing on the rocks
When marine iguanas are not diving for food, they bask in the sunshine around the coastline. The lizards' dark skin helps to absorb (take in) the Sun's heat.

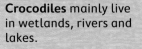

Crocodiles mainly live in wetlands, rivers and lakes.

Sneaky snake

The yellow-bellied sea snake has a sneaky trick. Once its colourful underside has attracted a fish, it darts backwards – so the fish is next to its open mouth, ready to be eaten.

Odd one out

Which of these creatures is cold blooded?

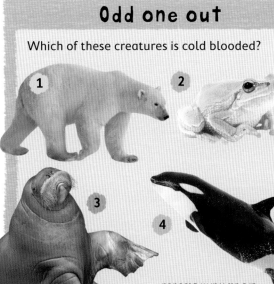

1

2

3

4

Answer 2 The frog. The others are all warm blooded

Sea turtles only come ashore to lay their eggs.

Looking for food

Banded sea snakes swim around coral reefs in search of their favourite food – eels.

Frogs rely on the sun to keep their body temperature up.

Deep-sea creatures

Few creatures can survive in the dark, icy-cold ocean depths. Food is so hard to find that some animals have unusual features, such as invisible teeth and their own fishing rods, to help them survive.

Lots of life
An amazing variety of life thrives in the deep sea near hot underwater vents.

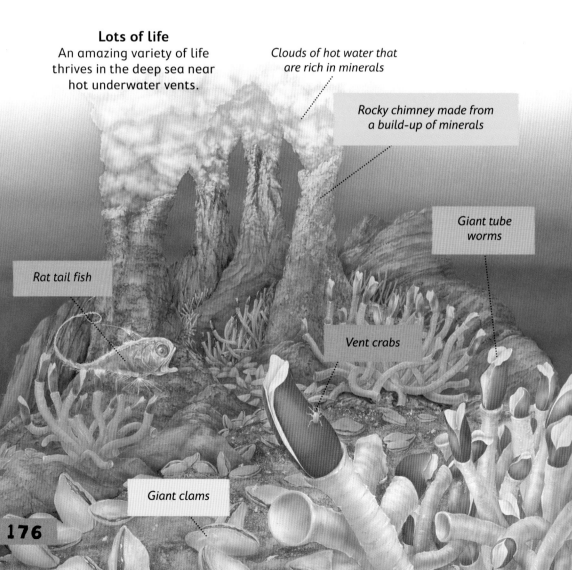

Clouds of hot water that are rich in minerals

Rocky chimney made from a build-up of minerals

Giant tube worms

Rat tail fish

Vent crabs

Giant clams

A **barreleye fish's** eyes are very sensitive, which helps it to spot its prey.

Monster of the deep

Giant squid grow up to 15 metres in length. They have long, powerful tentacles and huge eyes.

Giant isopods have long antennae, so they can feel their way in the dark.

In the dark

Fangtooth fish don't have good eyesight. Instead they can sense tiny movements in the water made by their prey.

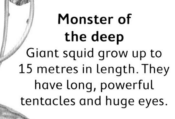

Gulper eels have enormous mouths for scooping up lots of prey in one mouthful.

Super swimmers

There are more than 21,000 different types of fish. Almost all of them are covered in scales and use fins and a muscular tail to power themselves through the water. They have slits called gills that take oxygen from the water so that they can breathe.

Ocean schools

A large group of fish is called a school or shoal. The fish are protected from hunters when there are such large numbers.

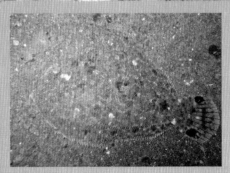

Hidden on the seabed

The shape and colour of flounders help to camouflage them on the seabed.

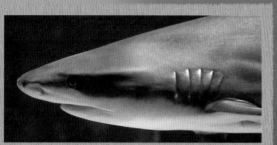

Breathing underwater

Fish have gills on each side of their head. As water flows across them, oxygen is taken into the fish's bloodstream.

Oarfish grow up to 8 metres long. Their length helps to protect them from hunters.

Sunfish were given their name because they like to sunbathe at the ocean surface.

FUN FACT!

Flying fish can use their winglike fins to keep them in the air for as long as 30 seconds!

Strong sharks

Sharks are meat eaters. Some filter tiny prey from the water, or lie in wait for victims on the seabed. Others speed through the ocean after prey.

Speedy swimmer
Great white sharks can speed through the water at 30 kilometres an hour.

Sharp teeth
Sharks have lots of slim, razor-sharp teeth. Different types of shark have teeth that are suited to what they eat.

Inside a shark

Sharks don't have bones. Their skeletons are made of a gristly substance called cartilage.

Dorsal fin helps the shark steer through the water

Ampullae of Lorenzini are used to sense electricity from nearby fish

Nostril

Jaw

Pectoral fin

Tail fin is used to push the shark through the water

Basking sharks eat huge amounts of tiny sea creatures called plankton.

Hammerhead sharks have a nostril and an eye on each end of their head.

Tiger sharks may produce as many as 40 babies at any one time.

Quiz time!

1 How long is an oarfish?

2 What is a group of fish called?

3 What are barnacles?

Q2 Picture clue

Answers **1** Up to 8 metres **2** School **3** Shellfish

181

Fast flippers

Seals, sea lions and walruses are warm-blooded mammals that have adapted to ocean life. They have flippers instead of legs and a streamlined body. Instead of fur, they have a layer of fat called blubber to keep them warm in cold waters.

Super swimmers

Leopard seals spend most of their lives in water and attack penguins when they swim and dive. They have long, sharp teeth to bite into the flesh of their prey.

Giant of the ocean

The male southern elephant seal is as big as a real elephant. It is almost 6 metres long and weighs about 5 tonnes.

Sea otters live around the Pacific coast among huge forests of seaweed.

Making noise

Sea lions get their name because they make a loud roaring sound. Unlike seals, they have ear flaps on their heads.

Walruses use their tusks to break breathing holes in the ice.

FUN FACT!

Leopard seals are noisy! They chirp and whistle in their sleep.

Great travellers

Many ocean animals migrate (travel) incredible distances every year. They have different reasons for doing this. Some travel to certain places for breeding. Others migrate south in the winter to reach warmer climates.

On the move
Loggerhead turtles are born on beaches in Japan. As soon as they have hatched from their eggs, they hurry to the sea and make a two-year journey to Mexico. They return to Japan to breed.

184

Round trip
Arctic terns can fly more than 40,000 kilometres in one year. They travel from breeding areas in the Arctic to the Antarctic, and back again, each year.

Salmon live in the ocean. They travel into rivers to lay their eggs.

Long journey
During the summer, humpback whales migrate to the icy waters in the north and south of the world. In winter, they breed in tropical waters.

Spiny lobsters travel in long columns by touch, using their long, spiky antennae (feelers).

Air aces

Many birds live near the ocean. Albatrosses
are the biggest seabirds. The wandering
albatross has a wingspan of about
3 metres. It is so large that it has
to take off by launching from a cliff.

Above the water
The southern royal albatross is the
second largest albatross, with a
wingspan of about 3 metres. It
mainly eats squid and fish.

Quiz time!

Match these seabirds to their correct names.

1 Herring gull

2 Cormorant

3 Arctic tern

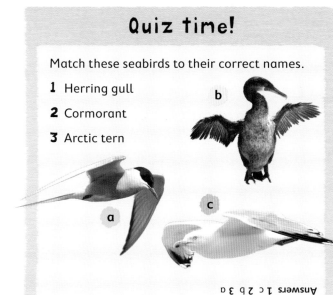

b

a

c

Answers 1 c 2 b 3 a

Gannets can dive into water to catch fish from a height of 30 metres.

Male frigate birds puff up their **red throat pouches** to show off to females.

Building nests
Many birds make nests on high cliff ledges. Puffins often make their own burrows, or they may take over an abandoned rabbit hole.

Boobies dance to show off their blue or red feet.

187

All kinds of penguin

There are 17 different types of penguin, mainly living in the Antarctic. Their black-and-white plumage is important camouflage. From above, the black back blends in with the water. From below, the white belly is difficult to see against the sunlit surface of the sea.

Good swimmers

Penguins can swim, but not fly. They have oily, waterproof feathers and flipper-like wings. Instead of lightweight, hollow bones – like a flying bird's – some penguins have solid heavy bones. This helps them to stay underwater longer when diving for food.

Word scramble!

Unscramble the letters to find four different words to do with penguins.

1 olmfagecau

2 insgw

3 ckihcs

4 dvnigi

Answers **1** camouflage **2** wings **3** chicks **4** diving

Adélie penguins build their nests from stones and small rocks.

Emperor penguin chicks keep warm by nestling in their father's chest feathers.

FUN FACT!

The fastest swimming bird is the gentoo penguin. It has been known to swim at a top speed of 27 kilometres an hour.

FANTASTIC MAMMALS

What are mammals?

There are thousands of mammals living on Earth. Some can swim, some can fly and all are warm-blooded. Being warm-blooded means that mammals can keep their body temperature the same in any weather conditions.

In the ocean
There are more than 35 different kinds of dolphin. The dusky dolphin likes to swim near boats, and can leap and somersault above the waves.

FUN FACT!

Dolphins can travel and feed in groups of up to 2000!

Pangolins are covered in hard scales for protection.

Red pandas sleep during the day and feed at night.

Motherly love

Orang-utans are the largest mammals to live in trees. Like all mammals, young orang-utans feed on their mother's milk.

Elephants on parade

You will need
paper • pens • scissors

1 Fold a long sheet of paper backwards and forwards into wide zigzags.

2 Draw an elephant shape onto the top page, with the tail joined to one edge and the trunk to the other.

3 Cut around the outline.

4 Draw ears and eyes onto each shape and colour them in. Open out your chain. All the elephants are holding trunks and tails!

Beavers have flat tails and webbed feet, making them excellent swimmers.

Mammal families

Some mammals live alone, except for when they have young. Other mammals like to live in groups. There are different names for these groups, depending on the animal.

Striped herd

Zebras live in groups called herds. There are 5 to 15 animals in a herd — several mothers and their babies, and one male stallion.

FANTASTIC MAMMALS

Animal group names

A troop
of chimps

A pack
of wolves

A harem
of seals

Lions live in groups called **prides**. All other big cats live alone.

Koalas live alone in trees. They eat the leaves of eucalyptus plants.

Meerkats live in large groups called colonies of up to 30 animals.

Baby mammals

Most mammals give birth to their babies but some, such as the duck-billed platypus, lay eggs. All baby mammals drink their mother's milk. It contains all the goodness they need to grow.

Spotty cubs
The female puma, or mountain lion, gives birth to cubs with spotted fur. The spots disappear as the cubs grow older.

FANTASTIC MAMMALS

Lots of babies

Virginia opossums have more babies than any other mammal – as many as 21.

Elephants have the **longest pregnancies** of any mammal – about 20 months.

Quiz time!

1 How many different types of dolphin are there?

2 Which animals live in a pride?

3 What is the biggest baby in the world?

4 Which animal has the longest pregnancy?

Q2 Picture clue

Answers 1 35 2 Lions 3 Blue whale 4 Elephant

A **baby gorilla** may stay with its mother for up to four years.

Biggest mammals

The blue whale is the biggest mammal in the world. It lives in the sea. It measures up to 33.5 metres in length – as long as seven family cars parked end to end. The elephant is the biggest land mammal, while the smallest mammal is the hog-nosed bat.

Mammal mix-up

You will need
pens • paper • friends

1 The first player draws the head of a mammal, giving it a long neck, then folds over the paper, so that only the neck shows, and passes it on.

2 Without looking under the fold, the next player adds a body to the neck, and folds the paper again.

3 The third player draws legs and feet and passes it to the last player. Unfold the paper. What a mix-up!

FANTASTIC MAMMALS

Mouse deers are the smallest deers — they are as small as hares.

Great giant
The blue whale is a true giant. It reaches up to 150 tonnes in weight — that's as heavy as 2000 adults or 35 elephants!

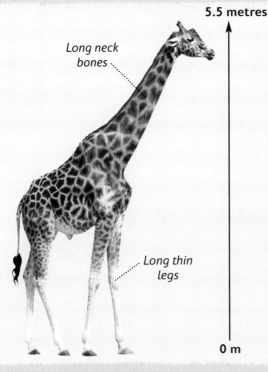

5.5 metres

Long neck bones

Long thin legs

0 m

Capybaras are the largest rodents in the world.

Pygmy shrews have such small eyes, they rely on their senses of smell and hearing.

Towering above
The giraffe is the tallest of all mammals. It reaches 5.5 metres in height — the same as three people standing on each other's shoulders.

Top racers

The cheetah can run faster than any other animal. It can reach speeds of 100 kilometres an hour, but it cannot run this fast for long. The cheetah hunts other fast-moving mammals, such as the brown hare or the pronghorn antelope.

Make a moving bear

You will need
pens • card • scissors • split pins

1 Draw two circles onto card, for the head and body. Add ears to the head and cut out the shapes.

2 Draw a face onto the head and colour in the bear.

3 Draw four legs. Cut them out and colour them in, too.

4 Push split pins through the tops of the legs into the body of the bear. Now your bear can move!

Flexible spine

Long tail for balance

Powerful leg muscles

Strong wrist bones

Built for speed

The cheetah's body has many features that help it to run really fast.

Pronghorns can only run at a speed of 70 kilometres an hour for a short time.

Brown hares have strong back legs to help them move quickly.

Chasing and catching

The cheetah's long slender legs and muscular body help it to quickly catch its prey, such as the pronghorn.

Red kangaroos can jump up to 10 metres in a single bound.

High fliers

Bats are the only true flying mammals. They zoom through the air on wings made of skin. Flying lemurs don't really fly – they just glide from tree to tree. Other gliding mammals include flying squirrels and gliders.

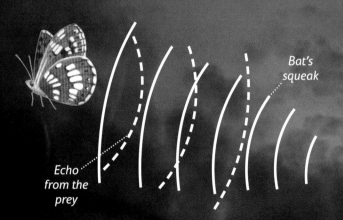

Bat's squeak

Echo from the prey

Hunting with sound

The bat uses echoes to hunt at night. It lets out a high-pitched squeak as it flies. When the sound waves hit an animal, they bounce back. The bat uses the echo to work out where its prey is.

Night-time hunters
Bats are small flying mammals that flit about at night after flying insects, such as butterflies. They grab their prey from the air while in flight.

Fruit bats eat their own weight in fruit each day.

The **vampire bat** feeds on small animals such as mice.

When gliding, the **American flying squirrel** uses its tail to steer.

FUN FACT!

A vampire bat only feeds on the blood of other mammals. It drinks about 26 litres of blood each year!

Champion diggers

Many mammals live underground. They need sharp claws and strong front paws to dig through the soil. Badgers dig a network of chambers and tunnels called a sett. There are special areas in the sett for breeding, sleeping and storing food.

Underground home
Badgers usually stay in the burrow during the day and come out at night. They line their sleeping areas with dry grass and leaves.

Armadillos use their sharp claws to dig for food and shelter.

Ready to dig

Moles have special front feet that are shaped like spades. This helps them to dig the underground tunnels where they live.

Ground squirrels have strong front paws to help them dig underground.

Finding food

Sloth bears have long claws, which are excellent for digging up ants and termites. They then use their strong lips to suck up the bugs one by one.

FUN FACT!

Badgers are playful animals — the adults are often seen enjoying a game of leapfrog with their cubs!

River mammals

Most river mammals spend only part of their time in water. Creatures such as the river otter and the water rat live on land and go into the water to find food. The hippopotamus, however, spends most of its day in water to keep cool.

Strong swimmer

Webbed feet help to push the water vole through the water.

Living in water

The water opossum dives into rivers to find fish. It has waterproof fur and webbed back feet.

FANTASTIC MAMMALS

Quiz time!

1 What is the biggest land mammal?

2 What type of mammal is a capybara?

3 Which mammal can run the fastest?

4 What do vampire bats feed on?

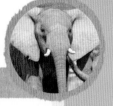

Q1 Picture clue

Answers 1 Elephant **2** Rodent **3** Cheetah **4** Blood

Manatees are water-living mammals that feed on plants.

In the depths
The platypus uses its duck-like beak to find food in the murky riverbed. It has webbed feet to help it swim through the water.

Hippos are not good swimmers. Instead, they walk on the riverbed.

Snow mammals

Mammals that live in very cold places, such as the Arctic and Antarctic, have thick fur to keep them warm. Also, the colour of their coats is very important. The polar bear, Arctic hare and snow leopard all have white fur to help them to hide in the snow.

Keeping warm
The polar bear is the biggest land mammal in the Arctic. Its thick fur helps to keep it warm in the cold conditions.

FUN FACT!

The polar bear needs its thick fur to keep out the Arctic cold — even the soles of its feet are furry!

Careful camouflage
The snow leopard lives in the mountains of central Asia. It has a grey coat, so it is difficult to see in the snow.

Male walruses have long teeth called tusks, for digging up shellfish from the seabed.

Musk oxen have long shaggy coats to help them to survive the Arctic cold.

Waterproof fur

Harp seals are surrounded by snow, ice and freezing cold water. Their thick, white fur is waterproof so they can dive into the sea to catch fish.

Snowshoe hares have brown coats in summer, which then turn white in winter.

Fins and flippers

Most swimming mammals have flippers and fins instead of legs. Seals and sea lions have paddle-like flippers. They use them to drag themselves along on land, as well as for swimming. Whales and dolphins never come onto land. They use their tails and flippers to swim.

Smooth swimmers
Many kinds of dolphin live in groups called schools. They have smooth skin to help them slip easily through the water.

Whale of a time!

You will need
long balloon • newspaper strips
papier-mâché paste • paints • paintbrush

1 Blow up a long balloon and tie a knot in the end.

2 Paste the newspaper strips onto the balloon. Repeat until the balloon has three layers of paper.

3 Leave it to dry for two days, then use a pin to pop the balloon.

4 Paint the whale blue and stick on paper fins and a tail.

The **grey whale** dives to the seafloor to feed using filters in its mouth called baleen.

Dolphins are energetic, and can often be seen leaping from the water.

Flipper

Amazing acrobatics

Humpback whales can weigh up to 30 tonnes, but they are able to leap out of the water using their powerful flippers and tail.

Killer whales are the largest members of the dolphin family.

In the rainforest

Rainforest mammals live at all levels of the forest, from the tallest trees to the forest floor. Bats fly over the tree tops and monkeys and apes swing from branch to branch. Lower down, smaller creatures, such as civets and pottos, hide among the thick greenery.

Down in the swamp
Jaguars live in the rainforests of Central and South America. They are strong swimmers, and can often be found in swampy areas.

Tops of the trees

The aye-aye is related to the lemur. It has an unusually long middle finger, so it can dig into trees and pull out grubs to eat.

Tapirs live on the rainforest floor and have long, bendy snouts.

Agoutis have strong teeth that can bite through hard nut shells.

Moving around

Ring-tailed lemurs only live on the island of Madagascar. In the rainforest, they walk along the ground and move through the trees.

FUN FACT!

The sloth spends so much time upside down that its fur grows downwards – the opposite way to most mammals. This is so rainwater drips off more easily.

213

Desert life

Mammals that live in the desert have developed ways to escape the scorching heat. The North African gerbil burrows underground and only comes out at night. Not all deserts are hot – the Gobi Desert in Asia can be cold during winter.

Keeping warm
The camel has thick fur to keep it warm during the Gobi Desert's cold winter.

FANTASTIC MAMMALS

The **desert kangaroo rat** comes out at night to find seeds.

Finding water
Wildebeest find areas where there is enough water to drink.

Hyenas are good hunters, and sometimes steal other animals' food.

Quiz time!

1 What is the biggest land mammal in the Arctic?

2 Which mammal can walk on riverbeds?

3 What are the walrus' long teeth called?

4 Where do ring-tailed lemurs live?

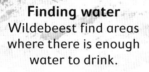

Q1 Picture clue

Fennec foxes have large ears to help them lose heat.

Answers 1 Polar bear 2 Hippopotamus 3 Tusks 4 Madagascar

Plant food

Plant eaters spend much of their time eating in order to get enough nourishment (goodness from food). The good side to being a plant eater is that the animal does not have to chase and fight for its food as hunters do.

Panda's plant
Nearly all of the panda's diet is bamboo. It eats fresh shoots in spring, mature leaves in summer and stems in winter.

Rabbits have strong teeth for eating leaves and bark.

Long tongue

The giraffe's black tongue is almost 30 centimetres long. It uses it to grip leaves and pull them into its mouth.

Rhinos can be heard munching on plants from 400 metres away.

Munching lemurs

Lemurs mainly eat plants. They live in tropical forests where there are lots of fresh leaves and ripe fruit all year round.

Wombats feed on the grass around their burrow.

Hungry hunters

Mammals that hunt and kill other creatures are called carnivores. Lions, tigers, wolves and dogs are all carnivores. Many carnivores do not have to hunt every day – one kill will last them for several days.

Meat and plants
Bears are carnivores, but many eat more plants than meat. In summer, brown bears wade into rivers and catch fish.

Practice makes perfect

The tiger is an expert hunter. Creeping up on its prey, such as deer, it pounces and kills its victim quickly.

Wolves hunt in packs, so they can kill larger animals.

Wild boars are related to farmyard pigs. They eat plants and small animals.

Cool cats!

You will need

scissors • paper plate • paints • paintbrush glue • paper • wool • elastic bands

1 Cut eye and nose holes in the plate.

2 Paint a cat face — maybe a tiger or a lion.

3 Stick on paper ears, and whiskers and a mane made from wool.

4 Make a hole through each side of the plate and loop elastic bands through the holes. Slip the bands over your ears and roar away!

Caracals can leap 3 metres into the air to catch a passing bird.

BRILLIANT BIRDS

What is a bird?

A bird has two legs, a pair of wings and
a body that is covered with feathers.
Birds live all over the world, from
icy Antarctica to the hottest deserts.

Safe and sound

All birds lay eggs
with a hard shell.
This protects the
growing young.
The parent birds keep
the eggs safe and
warm until the
chicks hatch.

New life
Once the chicks (baby birds)
hatch from their eggs, they
need to be fed regularly to
help them grow stronger.

222

Crown

Bill or beak

Breast

Made for flight
A bird's body is designed to help it fly. It has light, hollow bones and special flight feathers on its wings.

Back

Wing

Legs

Claw

Feet

Tail

Take off
Pigeons have strong wing muscles that help them to take off quickly and fly at speeds of up to 80 kilometres an hour.

Whistling swans are thought to have the most feathers of any bird – more than 25,000.

Ostriches have strong legs so they can run fast.

Hornbills have hornlike growths on their beaks called casques.

Bird species

There are more than 9000 different types, or species, of bird. Scientists have organized these species into groups called orders.

Birds of prey
The king vulture belongs to the same order as 290 other birds of prey (hunting birds) species. The king vulture is known for its bright colours.

Flamingos
Flamingos are very different from other types of bird. This means that they are the only species in their order.

224

Game birds
This large order includes turkeys, chickens and pheasants. Game birds do not normally fly. Instead they walk or run to get around.

Goshawks are birds of prey. They can kill animals as big as rabbits.

There are 18 species of **penguin**. Most of these live in Antarctica.

FUN FACT!
Bird brains aren't stupid — ravens and pigeons can work out simple sums, while parrots can copy human speech!

Perching birds
The largest order is the perching birds, which includes robins. Robins can be recognized by their red chest feathers.

Biggest and smallest

The largest bird in the world is the ostrich. It is almost 3 metres tall and weighs up to 115 kilograms – twice as much as an average adult human. The smallest bird is the tiny bee hummingbird, which is only about 5 centimetres long.

Great speed

Ostriches live in the grasslands of Africa. They are the world's fastest two-legged runners and can reach a speed of 50 kilometres an hour.

Longest wings
Wandering albatrosses spend most of their time in the air. They have the longest wings of any bird – up to 3 metres from tip to tip.

FUN FACT!

Bee hummingbirds are 5 centimetres long and weigh only 2 grams.

Andean condors are the largest birds of prey at 110 centimetres long.

Measuring size

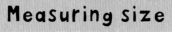

You will need
measuring tape

1 Measure your height from your foot to your head. Then measure your armspan from the tip of one hand to the tip of the other.

2 Compare these to the measurements on this page. If you stood next to an ostrich, how much taller would it be? Would a wandering albatross have longer wings than your arms?

Collared falconets are the smallest birds of prey at only 19 centimetres long.

227

Starting life

A bird's egg protects the chick growing inside. The yellow yolk provides the baby bird with food. Layers of egg white cushion the chick. The hard shell keeps the chick safe. The shell is porous – it allows air in and out so the chick can breathe.

Time to hatch
When it is ready to hatch, the chick chips away at the egg shell and breaks free.

3 *The egg splits wide open*

1 *The chick starts to crack the egg*

2 *The chick uses its egg tooth to break the shell*

4 *The chick is able to wriggle free. Its parents will look after it for several weeks until it can care for itself*

Chicks have a small lump on their beaks called an **egg tooth.**

Emperor penguins only have one baby each year.

On a cliff
Guillemots live on cliff tops. They do not build nests, but simply lay their eggs on the rock or bare earth.

Keeping eggs warm
Parent birds, such as the emu, take turns to sit on the eggs to keep them warm. This is called incubation.

FUN FACT!

The guillemot's egg is pear-shaped, so that if the egg is pushed or knocked, it does not roll off the cliff.

Family life

Each species of bird has its own way of caring for its young. Some birds such as Emperor penguins rear (bring up) their young. Other birds, such as ducks and geese, have young that find their own food as soon as they hatch.

Follow the leader
Ducklings follow the first moving thing they see when they hatch — usually their mother.

FUN FACT!

Penguins huddle together for warmth while they incubate their eggs. They take it in turns to stand on the outside of the group to take the force of the cold winds.

Swans carry their young, called **cygnets**, on their backs as they swim.

A safe place

Woodpeckers make their nests in holes that they have dug out of tree trunks. The chicks need a lot of care from their parents before they are ready to leave the safety of the nest.

Desert bird

The sandgrouse has special feathers on its tummy that soak up water. It carries water back to its chicks when they are too small to fly.

Owls usually lay up to seven eggs at a time. The chicks are called owlets.

Bird homes

Birds make nests in which to lay their eggs and keep them safe. Nests can be made of twigs, leaves, mud or saliva. They are built in a variety of places, such as trees, near water or in the walls of buildings.

The biggest nest
The bald eagle makes one of the biggest nests of any bird. It is made of sticks and built in a tree or on rocks.

232

Hanging home

The male weaver bird makes a nest from grass and stems. He knots and weaves the pieces together to make a long nest, which hangs from the branch of a tree.

Swallows often make their nests in the eaves of buildings, near the roof.

Cuckoos don't make their own nests. Instead, they lay eggs in other birds' nests.

1 *The male weaver bird twists strips of leaves around a branch or twig*

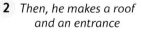

2 *Then, he makes a roof and an entrance*

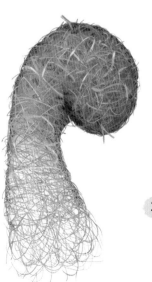

FUN FACT!

Sometimes people collect the nests of cave swiftlets to make bird's nest soup!

3 *When the nest is finished, the long entrance helps to provide a safe shelter for the eggs*

Fast fliers

The fastest flying bird is the peregrine falcon.
It hunts other birds in the air and makes
amazing high-speed dives to catch its prey.
Ducks and geese are also fast fliers. The eider
duck can reach speeds of more than
65 kilometres an hour.

Powerful dive
When it makes a dive, the
peregrine falcon pushes itself
down towards the ground.
This is called a stoop.

Make a bird cake

You will need
225 g of suet, lard or dripping • 500 g of seeds
or nuts • empty yogurt pot • string • pan

1 Ask an adult for help. Melt the fat in a pan on
a low heat and mix it with the seeds or nuts.

2 Pour the mixture into the yogurt pot and
leave it to cool.

3 Remove the cake from the pot. Make a hole
through the cake and put a string through
the hole. Hang it from a tree outside and
watch the birds eat the yummy treat!

Roadrunners can fly,
but they prefer to walk
or run.

Beating wings
Hummingbirds beat
their wings more than
50 times a second as
they hover in the air.

Mergansers are ducks
that can dive very
quickly into the water
to catch fish.

Swallows twist and
zigzag in the air as
they fly.

Swimmers and divers

Penguins are the best swimmers and divers in the bird world. They spend most of their lives in water, using their wings as strong flippers to help them swim.

Long dives
Emperor penguins can dive for more than 18 minutes. Their tail and webbed feet help them steer through the water.

Quiz time!

1 How many types of bird are there?

2 What is the hornlike growth on a hornbill's beak called?

3 Which bird has the longest wings?

4 What is another name for a hunting bird?

Q3 Picture clue

Answers 1 More than 9000 **2** Casque **3** Wandering albatross **4** Bird of prey

Short dives

Arctic terns catch fish and other creatures by making short dives into the water.

FUN FACT!

The gentoo penguin is one of the fastest swimming birds. It can swim faster than most people can run!

Northern gannets dive from great heights to catch fish from the sea.

Upside down

Some types of duck find food by turning themselves upside down to search under the surface of the water.

Eagles are very skilled at plucking fish from the water.

237

Night birds

Some birds hunt at night, when there is less competition for prey. These birds have special ways of finding their way in the dark. They might have a strong sense of smell or sensitive eyesight.

Roly-poly owl!

You will need

scissors • empty yogurt pot • drinking straw
empty cotton reel • coloured paper • glue

1 Make two small holes at the top of the yogurt pot. Push a drinking straw through one of side of the pot, through the centre of the cotton reel and out through the other hole.

2 Cut out eyes, wings and a beak from coloured paper and stick them onto the pot. Now roll your owl around!

Poorwills hunt at night by opening their beaks wide to snap insects out of the air.

Kiwis have a good sense of smell, which helps them to find food.

Strong senses
Barn owls have large, sensitive eyes to help them see in the dark. They also have very good hearing.

The **kakapo** is the only parrot that is active at night.

239

Feeding time

All birds have a beak for eating. They have different kinds of beak, suited to the types of food they eat. Insect-eating birds have thin, sharp beaks for picking up tiny prey. Hunting birds have hooked beaks for tearing flesh.

Eating insects

The European bee-eater uses its sharp beak to catch bees, wasps and dragonflies. Once it has snapped up an insect, it rubs its catch on a branch to get rid of the sting.

Eggs for dinner

The Egyptian vulture steals other birds' eggs. It cracks the eggs by dropping them on the ground or by dropping stones on them.

Hummingbirds use their long tongues to sip the nectar inside flowers.

A nutty treat
Nuthatches feed on nuts and seeds as well as some insects. They have a long pointed beak and can hang upside down so they can easily get at food.

Vultures have bald heads so they don't get messy when eating dead animals.

Fish food
Puffins have large colourful beaks, which can hold 12 or more fish. This is very useful, as puffins fill their beaks and carry the food back to their young.

Oxpeckers pull ticks from the skin of animals such as antelopes.

Fierce hunters

Eagles, hawks and owls are all birds of prey – birds that hunt other animals. The golden eagle is one of the fiercest birds of prey. When it spies a victim, the golden eagle dives down and seizes the prey in its powerful claws, called talons.

Hunting snakes

Secretary birds are not like other birds of prey. They hunt snakes by stamping on them using their long, powerful legs.

Food on the wing

Philippine eagles hunt from perches. They eat lots of different animals, such as flying lemurs, monkeys, bats and snakes. Philippine eagles are very rare, and are protected by law.

242

Bald eagles swoop down and seize fish in their sharp claws.

Ravens mainly hunt rats and mice, but they can catch larger animals, such as rabbits.

Use your feet!

You will need
different sized objects such as pencils, coins and books

1 Get your friends together to see if you can pick things up using your feet – just like an eagle.

2 Start with the easiest object, such as a pencil. Make the objects harder and harder to pick up with your feet. Whoever can pick up the most objects is the winner!

Most **hawks** are useful to humans because they hunt rodents that damage crops.

243

Rainforest birds

Rainforests are home to a huge variety of bird life. One-fifth of all the birds in the world live in the Amazon rainforest, in South America. Birds of paradise are very colourful. They live in the rainforests of Australia and New Guinea.

Bright colours

The scarlet macaw is named after its bright-red feathers. It lives in the tropical forests of South America, feeding on fruits and seeds.

A rare sight

The blue bird of paradise is very rare and can only be found in New Guinea and northeastern Australia.

244

Quetzals' tail feathers grow up to 90 centimetres long.

Powerful beak
Found in the South American rainforests, the hyacinth macaw has a very powerful beak to crack open hard nuts and seeds.

Toucans all have large, brightly coloured beaks to help attract mates.

Quiz time!

1 What are a bird of prey's claws called?

2 Which parrot is active at night?

3 What do hummingbirds eat?

4 Where do one-fifth of the world's birds live?

Q2 Picture clue

Answers 1 Talons **2** Kakapo **3** Nectar **4** Amazon rainforest

Rainbow lorikeets feed high up in the rainforest canopy.

Snow birds

The coldest places on Earth are the Arctic and the Antarctic. Here it is too cold for most birds to live all year round. In the Antarctic, most of the land is always covered in ice.

Life on ice
Penguins live in the Antarctic. They have a thick layer of fat under their skin to protect them from the cold.

Arctic hunting

The snowy owl is the biggest hunting bird of the Arctic region. Snowy owls make their nests on the ground, among stones and moss.

The ptarmigan has white feathers to help it hide from enemies.

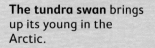

The snow bunting lives and breeds on islands around the Antarctic.

Handy penguins

You will need
black sock • cotton • glue • white cloth buttons • card • scissors

1 Glue the piece of white cloth to the black sock to make its chest feathers.

2 Make a beak out of card and attach it to the sock with some cotton. Stick on button eyes.

3 Cut holes in either side and push your hand into the sock, using your fingers as flippers.

The tundra swan brings up its young in the Arctic.

River life

Many birds live near rivers, lakes and marshes.
There are plenty of fish, insects and plants
to eat and places to nest.

Watching the water
The kingfisher perches on a branch
along streams and riverbanks,
watching for any signs of movement
of fish in the water. Then it swoops
down to catch its prey.

Fast dippers
The dipper lives
around fast-flowing
streams and can swim
and dive well.

Wading birds

Storks are wading birds, so they have long, spindly legs and a long beak for plucking fish from the water. Some storks also eat other creatures such as frogs and insects.

Herons stand in shallow water and grab their prey with their sharp beaks.

Pelicans collect fish in the big pouch that hangs beneath their long beaks.

Walking on water

Jacanas have long toes, so they can walk on lily pads that float on the water.

Ospreys are found near rivers and lakes. They feed mainly on fish.

249

AWESOME BUGS

What is a bug?

If a creepy-crawly has six legs, it is an insect.
If it has more legs or none at all, then it is
another kind of animal. The young of some
insects have no legs until they become adults.

Common fly
Houseflies are one of the
most common insects. They
feed on liquid food with
sponge-like mouthparts.

*Sticky pads and sharp
claws help houseflies
walk upside down*

Tiny ticks
Ticks have eight legs so
they are arachnids, not
insects. They feed on both
animal and human blood.

252

Snails are molluscs. They have hard shells to protect their soft bodies.

Shiny black or chestnut-brown in colour

About 18 pairs of legs

Body in pieces
Pill millipedes belong to the myriapod animal group. Their bodies have 12 segments.

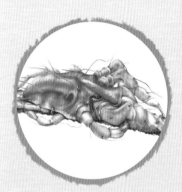

Mites belong to the arachnid family along with spiders and ticks.

Tail

Wriggly worms
Worms have soft bodies without legs. Their bodies are split into many segments. There are more than one million species of worm.

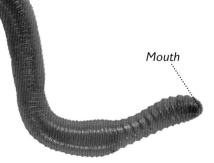

Segmented body

Mouth

Millipedes have up to 400 pairs of legs and, like centipedes, belong to the myriapod animal group.

The insect world

Insects form the largest of all animal groups, with millions of different kinds, or species. They are found almost everywhere in the world. Common insects include flies, ladybirds, butterflies, ants and bees.

Some holes in the nest contain honey the bees have made from flower nectar and pollen

Making honey
Honeybees live in nests called hives. They share jobs such as finding food, cleaning the nest and caring for young.

254

Cockchafer beetles can be found in woodland, farmland and gardens.

Colourful beetles

Ladybird beetles have round bodies. They are brightly coloured to put off predators.

Male **scorpionflies** have a harmless sting on a long, curved tail.

A bees' nest has hundreds of six-sided holes with wax walls

Earwigs live in dark, damp corners. They are mostly active at night.

Insect homes

Some insects live together in huge groups called colonies. There are four main types of insect that build large nests — termites, bees, wasps and ants.

Cutting leaves
Leafcutter ants bite off pieces of leaves and carry them to their nest. Here, they chew the leaves into a pile of mush, which rots and grows a type of fungus that the ants like to eat.

Paper nests
Some wasps build nests of paper, made from chewed-up bits of plants and wood.

Termites make their nests inside huge piles of mud and earth.

Cave crickets like to live in caves and other dark, damp places.

Quiz time!

1 How many legs does an insect have?

2 Is a snail an insect?

3 When are crickets mainly active?

4 What do some wasps make their nests out of?

Q2 Picture clue

Answers: **1** Six **2** No, a snail is a mollusc **3** At night **4** Paper

Ants build large, complex nests either on or under the ground.

Taking flight

Many insects can fly. The wings are attached to the middle part of their body, called the thorax. Most insects have two pairs of wings.

The hard outer wings are called elytra. They are red with black spots

The outer wings part to reveal the soft, flying wings underneath

Special wings
Ladybirds fly using their soft inner wings. They fly to look for food, to find new homes and to escape danger.

Up and away!

You will need
an adult • scissors • sticky tape
stiff card • tissue paper

1 Carefully fold the stiff card to make a cube-shaped box with two open ends.

2 Attach strips of stiff card to the sides to make struts for the wings. Make the wings from tissue paper and attach to the main box and the struts.

3 Hold the box as shown. Move the top and bottom walls in, then out. This bends the side walls to make the wings flap.

Apollo butterflies are strong fliers. They can fly to the top of mountains.

Fireflies are actually beetles. They flash bright lights to attract mates.

Huge compound eyes cover the entire head

Two pairs of veined wings

Long, slender body

Fast flier
The dragonfly is a fast, fierce hunter of mosquitoes, flies and other small insects.

Mosquitoes are small, widespread flies with scaly wings.

Hop, skip and jump

Many insects move around by hopping and jumping, rather than flying. They have long, strong legs and can leap great distances. This helps them to escape from enemies.

Leaping to safety
Grasshoppers have six legs and a pair of large wings. They prefer to escape from danger by leaping rather than flying.

Quiz time!

1 Which flying insect has scaly wings?

2 Which insect can jump more than 3 metres?

3 Which part of their body do springtails use to jump?

4 Are mites insects?

Q4 Picture clue

Answers 1 Mosquito 2 Grasshopper 3 Tail 4 No, arachnids

AWESOME BUGS

Crickets are all born with wings, but some cannot fly and only hop from place to place.

Long jump
Leafhoppers are strong fliers, but they can also jump great distances.

Powerful spring
Grasshoppers have very long back legs. Some types can jump more than 3 metres.

Fleas are tiny insects, but they can jump over 30 centimetres in length.

FUN FACT!
Click beetles can flick themselves an amazing 25 centimetres up into the air.

261

Speedy bugs

Some insects rarely jump or fly.
Instead, they prefer to run.
Cockroaches are champion sprinters
– they scurry speedily across the
ground on long legs.

Fast and low
Cockroaches have low, flat bodies.
They can run extremely fast into
narrow cracks in walls and floors.

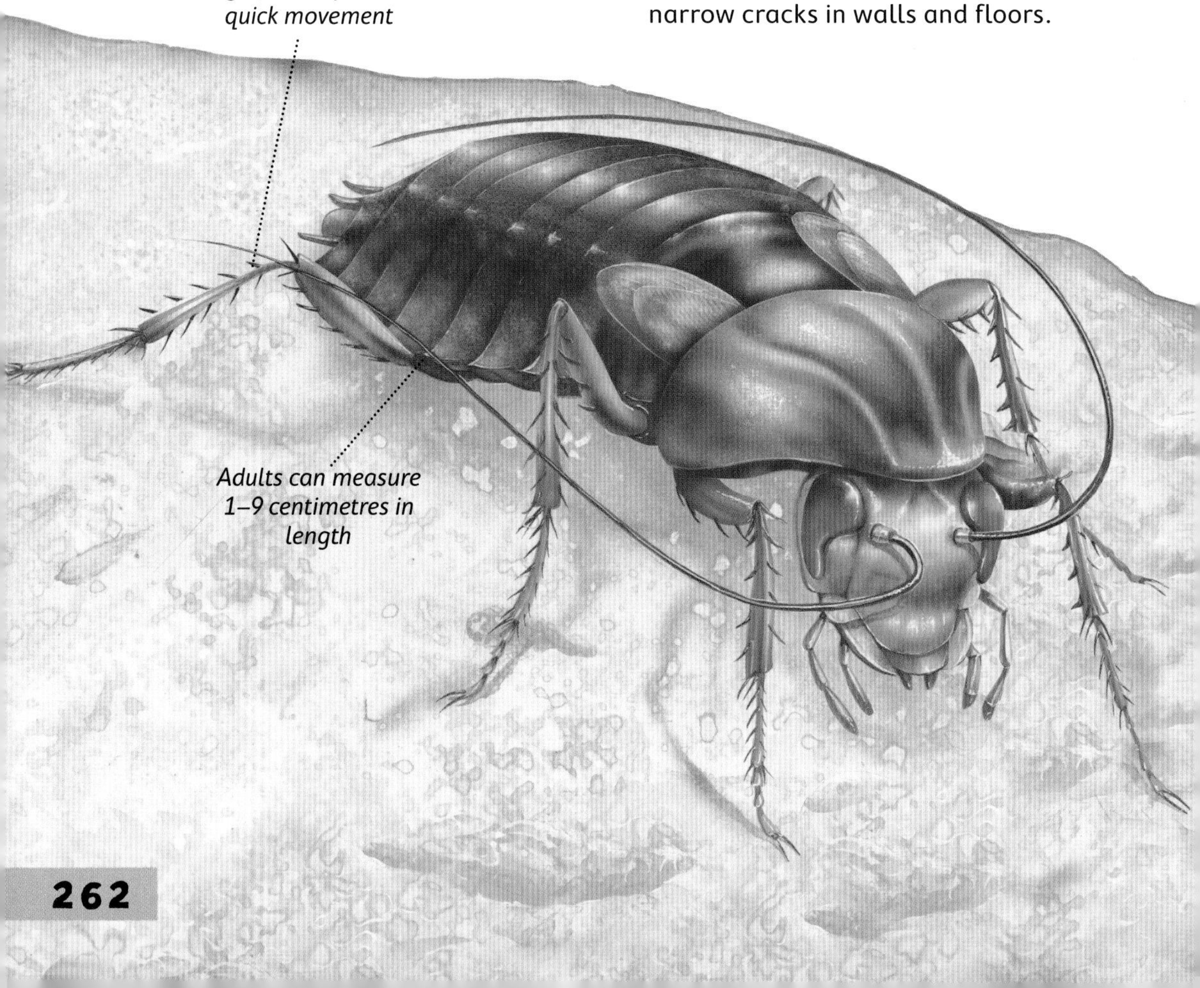

*Legs are adapted for
quick movement*

*Adults can measure
1–9 centimetres in
length*

262

Speed walker
The devil's coach-horse beetle walks long distances to find food.

Oriental cockroaches are found in dark, damp places such as drains and kitchen sinks.

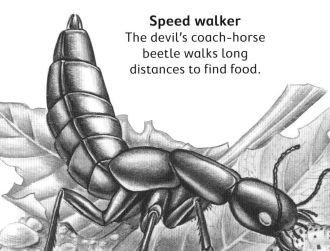

Hissing cockroaches are named after the loud hissing sound they make when they breathe.

In the water
Stonefly nymphs run around on riverbeds searching for food.

FUN FACT!

For its size, a green tiger beetle runs ten times as fast as a person! It runs about 60 to 70 centimetres a second. That is like a human sprinter running 100 metres in one second!

263

Swimmers and skaters

Many insects live underwater in ponds, streams, rivers and lakes. Some walk about on the bottom, while others use their legs to propel themselves through the water.

Expert swimmer
Diving beetles cannot breathe underwater. They have to come back up to the surface for air.

Mayfly nymphs have tails with feathery gills that allow them to breathe underwater.

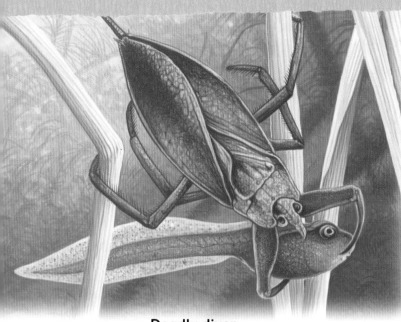

Deadly diver
Water scorpions live at the water's edge. They keep still and wait to pounce on tadpoles and other small water animals.

Pondskaters are slim and light so they can easily walk on water.

Skimming the surface
Water boatmen live in ponds, canals and ditches. They have strong legs, which help them move through the water.

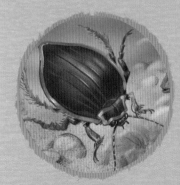

Great diving beetles enter the water to hunt tadpoles and baby fish.

Burrowing bugs

The soil is full of millions of creepy-crawlies.
Some are the young forms of insects, called
larvae or grubs. Others are fully grown insects.

Digging down
Earwigs live in soil and dig deep
tunnels to escape the cold weather.
They hide from predators in the dark.

Tiny burrower
Diplurans bury themselves in the soil. They feed on rotting plants and tiny insects.

Cranefly larvae are also called leatherjackets after their tough, leathery bodies.

Cicada larvae may live underground for more than ten years before they become adults.

Cranefly larvae stay underground, feeding on plant parts for up to five years.

Bugs and beetles

You will need
glue • paintbrush • paints • pipe cleaners
sticky tape • tissue paper

1 Screw up the tissue paper into a tight ball.

2 Wrap the ball with another piece of tissue paper and hold it together with sticky tape.

3 Paint on eyes and tape on pipe cleaners for legs. For a ladybird, paint the body red with black spots. For a bee, paint the body yellow with black stripes.

267

Bites and stings

Insects may be small, but they are fierce hunters. Many have mouthparts shaped like spears or saws, which they use for grabbing and tearing up their prey. Some have powerful bites and poisonous stings.

Snap and bite
The praying mantis is one of the most powerful insect hunters. Its front legs have sharp spines that snap together to grab prey.

Pierce and paralyze
The red-banded sand wasp uses its strong jaws to pierce its prey's thin skin. It then injects poison to paralyze its victim.

Lacewing larvae have jaws that suck body fluids out of their prey.

Quiz time!

1 What kind of insect is the devil's coach-horse?

2 Which insect is the fastest runner?

3 How many times can a honeybee sting before it dies?

4 Which insect can walk on water?

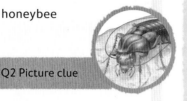

Q2 Picture clue

Answers 1 Beetle 2 Cockroach 3 Once 4 Pondskater

Bombardier beetles can squirt out a hot, toxic liquid to burn predators.

············ *Sting*

One sting
Bees can only use their sting once. They die soon after because the jagged sting remains stuck in their victim. This pulls out the bee's insides.

Hornets are a type of large wasp with very painful stings.

269

Hide and seek

Many insects are coloured or patterned to blend in with their natural surroundings. This is called 'camouflage'. It helps insects hide from hunters and allows predators to sneak up on prey, unseen.

Walking leaves
Leaf insects are leafy-green in colour and are very hard to spot among foliage.

Hard to spot

Stick insects are excellent at camouflaging themselves, especially when they keep still or sway with the wind.

Now you see me...

You will need
card • cardboard • glue • paints • scissors

1 Carefully cut out a butterfly shape from stiff card. Colour it brightly with a bold pattern.

2 Cut out leaf shapes from card. Colour them using the same colours as your butterfly. Make a branch using the cardboard and stick the leaves on top.

3 Put the butterfly on top of the leafy branch to see how it becomes camouflaged.

Moths often have similar colours and patterns as tree bark and dead leaf litter.

Shieldbugs have broad, flat bodies that look like the leaves around them.

Geometrid caterpillars have a brown, stick-like appearance.

Leafy wings
The brimstone butterfly looks just like a leaf. When it rests or feeds on a flower, it blends in with the plant.

Dinner time

Almost all insects eat plants. They feed on the sap (liquid) in stems and leaves, the nectar in flowers and the soft flesh of fruits and berries.

Stinky meal
Dung beetles roll animal droppings into big, round balls. They roll the balls into their nests and feed on them.

Nibbling wood

Termites feed on decaying wood, tree stumps and the roots of plants.

Furniture beetles like to eat the dead parts of trees and wood.

Death's head hawk-moth caterpillars feed on potato plants and tomato leaves.

FUN FACT!

Many insect species eat animal droppings. Some beetles lay their eggs in droppings, then the larvae hatch out and eat the dung!

Sap feeder

Spittlebugs are also known as froghoppers due to their frog-like appearance. They feed on plant sap.

Eight-legged creatures

Creepy-crawlies that have eight legs belong to the arachnid animal group. This includes spiders, mites, scorpions and ticks.

Pinch and sting
Scorpions have a poisonous sting at the tip of their tail. They grab their prey with their pincers then inject poison to kill it.

AWESOME BUGS

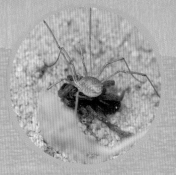

Harvestmen catch prey using their hooked claws.

Harmless tail
The horseshoe crab has a long, spiky tail, but it doesn't contain any venom.

Tarantulas such as the cobalt blue sink their fangs into prey to kill it.

Deadly bite
Sydney funnel webs are found in Australia. Their bite is highly venomous.

Ticks measure just 3 millimetres in length.

What is a spider?

A spider is an arachnid. All spiders are expert hunters — they have fangs to grab and inject poison into prey. There are around 40,000 species of spiders in the world.

Spider anatomy
Spiders usually have eight eyes, eight legs, and are venomous. Their bodies are made up of two parts — the cephalothorax (head and thorax) and the abdomen (body).

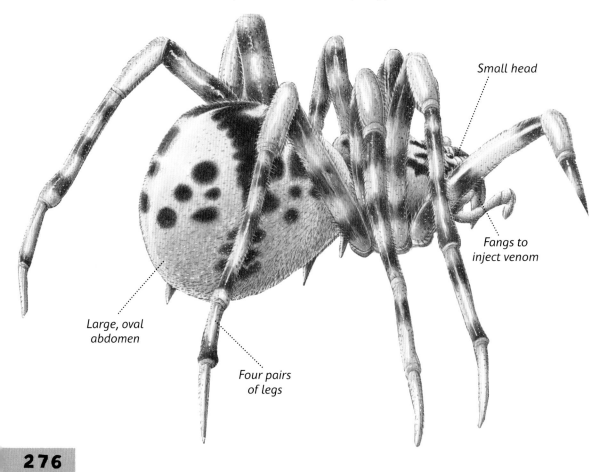

Small head

Fangs to inject venom

Large, oval abdomen

Four pairs of legs

Make a spider's web

You will need
an adult • card • cotton • PVA glue • scissors

1 Cut a large, circular hole out of the middle of the card. Stretch a piece of cotton from one edge of the circle to the other, and glue to both sides.

2 Do the same again several times at different angles. Make sure all the threads cross at the centre of the hole.

3 Starting at the centre, glue a long piece of thread to each of the threads. Work your way round in a spiral until you reach the edge. This is how a spider makes a web.

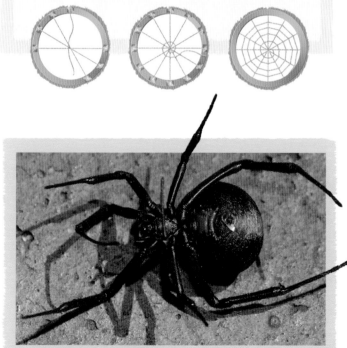

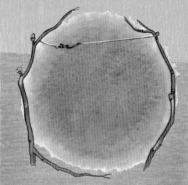

Stage 1
A spider starts a web by building a bridge.

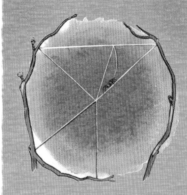

Stage 2
More threads are added to make a strong framework.

Stage 3
The spider fills the frame with circular threads.

Tiny killer

The Australian redback spider belongs to the most deadly group of spiders – the widow spiders.

277

Spider attacks

Not all spiders catch their prey using webs. Some chase their prey, while others hide until a suitable meal passes by.

Sharp fangs
The king baboon tarantula injects venom into small animals, such as mice.

Crab spiders can change colour to blend in with their surrounding and sneak up on prey.

Sticky weapon

The spitting spider has silk glands that are connected to poisonous fangs. When it spots its prey, it spits a sticky silk over the prey to catch it.

Toxic bite

Black widow spiders live in warm countries. They kill their prey by wrapping them in thread and injecting them with a strong venom.

Wolf spiders do not spin webs, they lie in wait and pounce on their victims.

FUN FACT!

Tarantulas are huge spiders from South America and Africa. Stretch your hand out and it still would not be as big as some of these giants!

All about legs

Centipedes and millipedes have hundreds of legs and belong to the myriapod group. Worms, snails and slugs have no legs, so they are not insects. They get around by sliding their bodies along the ground.

Slither and slime

Snails and slugs have no legs. They leave slimy trails wherever they have been. The slime is used for protection and to create a smooth surface for movement.

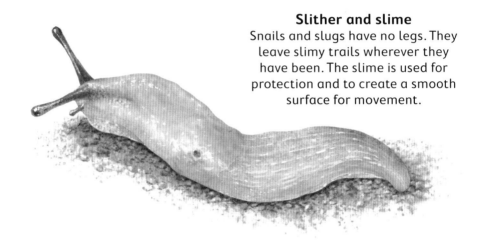

Burrowing deep down

Earthworms are good for soil. When they burrow into the ground, extra air gets to the roots of plants, helping them to grow.

Make a wormery

You will need
leaves • sand • see-through container • soil • worms

1 In a see-through container, put a 5-centimetre layer of sand and then a 5-centimetre layer of soil. Alternate the sand and soil until your container is almost full. Add leaves to the top.

2 Add some worms from your garden to the container, and keep it in a cool, dark place.

3 Every few days, see how the worms mix up the layers. Carefully put the worms back where you found them when you've finished.

Leeches have suckers at the end of their bodies for sucking blood.

The **Giant African millipede** can grow up to 28 centimetres long.

Fierce hunters
Centipedes are predators. They use their poisonous jaw-like claws to grab and kill their prey, including insects and spiders.

When disturbed, **pill millipedes** curl into a ball to protect themselves.

ANCIENT EGYPT

Life on the Nile

Without the river Nile, Egyptian
civilization might never have existed.
The Nile provided water for transport,
drinking and watering crops.

Water was taken from the Nile
using a shaduf – a wooden
bucket hanging from a long pole

Blocks of stone for the
pyramids were carried
across the river

Papyrus reeds had many
uses, including making
boats and shoes

Hunters caught hippos in the Nile.

Living on the Nile
Every year, the river flooded, making the land nearby fertile. Most Egyptians lived on the banks of the river so they could grow crops.

Temples were built to worship the Egyptian gods

Houses were built with mud from the river.

People spread further along the Nile as Egypt became more powerful.

Boats were the best way to get around in Egypt

Powerful pharaohs

The rulers of ancient Egypt were called pharaohs. Ordinary people believed that they were gods. The pharaoh was the most important and powerful person in the country.

Who's in charge

Officials called viziers helped the pharaoh to rule Egypt. Each ruler chose two viziers. They were very powerful and important men.

Quiz time!

1 Who was crowned pharaoh in 1473 BC?

2 What is the name of the river that runs through Egypt?

3 How did Egyptians travel?

4 What did people believe pharaohs really were?

Q3 Picture clue

Answers 1 Hatshepsut 2 Nile 3 By boat 4 Gods

Queen Hatshepsut

Hatshepsut was crowned pharaoh in 1473 BC when her husband, Thutmose II, died. She adopted the royal symbols of the double crown, the crook, the flail (whip) — and also the ceremonial beard!

Ramses II ruled for more than 60 years. He was a great builder and a brave soldier.

The pharaoh holds a hook and flail. They represent his power

Jewelled falcons represented the sun god and were worn by the pharaohs.

FUN FACT!

Women courtiers sometimes wore hair cones made of animal fat. The melting fat trickled down their heads, making their hair smell sweet, but look greasy!

Gods and goddesses

The ancient Egyptians worshipped more than 1000 different gods and goddesses. The most important was Ra, the sun god. A god was often shown as an animal, or half-human, half-animal.

King of the gods

At night, the sun god Ra travelled through the underworld and was born again each morning. According to the Egyptians, this was the reason the Sun rose each day.

Design a wall painting

You will need
pens • card • paints

1 Draw your own gods and goddesses. You can add crowns, wings, masks — anything you want.

2 Paint them lots of bright colours.

3 Hang the painting on your wall.

Horus was the god of the sky. He had the head of a falcon.

The underworld

Osiris was the god of the dead. He and his wife Isis were in charge of the underworld. Ancient Egyptians believed that dead people travelled to the underworld.

Sobek was a god of the river Nile.

Jackal-headed god

Anubis was in charge of preparing bodies to be mummified. As jackals were often found near cemeteries, Anubis was given the head of a jackal.

Tawaret represented mothers and young children.

289

The pyramids of Giza

The three pyramids at Giza are more than 4500 years old. They were built for three kings — Khufu, Khafre and Menkaure. After they died, their bodies were preserved as mummies and buried inside the pyramids.

The finished pyramids had a white coating to protect the stones underneath

Blocks of stone were moved by wooden sledges

The workers were given lots of water while working in the hot desert

The biggest pyramid
The Great Pyramid is the biggest pyramid in the world. It was built with more than two million blocks.

The huge stones were levered into exactly the right position

Teams of workers pulled the stones up the slopes

The **Great Sphinx at Giza** has the body of a lion and the head of a human.

Breaking in
Tomb robbers broke into the pyramids to steal the treasures that were buried with the pharaohs.

The **Step Pyramid** is one of the world's oldest pyramids.

Temples and tombs

The ancient Egyptians built magnificent buildings, including temples and tombs. From 2150 BC, pharaohs were not buried in pyramids, but in tombs in the Valley of the Kings. Gods such as Ra were worshipped in temples.

Quiz time!

1 What is the biggest pyramid called?

2 The Great Sphinx has the head of a human and the body of a – what?

3 Which god has the head of a jackal?

Q2 Picture clue

Answers 1 The Great Pyramid 2 Lion 3 Anubis

In 1922 the **death mask** of Tutankhamun was found in the Valley of the Kings.

The riches in the **Valley of the Kings** attracted many tomb robbers.

The **Great Hall at Karnak** has 134 papyrus columns that are up to 21 metres tall.

The temple of Osiris
The temple at Abu Simbel is carved out of sandstone rock. Four enormous statues of Ramses II guard the entrance. They are more than 20 metres high.

Preserving the dead

Making a mummy was skilled work. The body's
insides were removed, except for the heart.
Next, the body was left to dry for 40 days.
Then it was washed and filled with linen to keep
its shape. Finally, the body was covered in oil
and wrapped in linen bandages.

*Canopic jars were
used to store the dead
person's body parts*

Make a death mask

You will need
play mask • PVA glue • newspaper
paintbrush • paints

1 Cover the mask in PVA glue.

2 Tear the newspaper into strips. Layer the strips
over the mask and leave to dry.

3 Cover the mask with white paint. Leave to dry.

4 Use the paints to create your own death mask!

The priest wore a jackal mask to look like the god Anubis

Natron covered the body

Wrapping the body in bandages took eleven days.

Pets were made into mummies too.

Drying the body
The body was covered in natron, a kind of salt, to dry it out. Mummification was believed to protect the body when it was put in the tomb.

The **mummy** was placed in a special case to be buried.

295

War and weapons

Egypt had a professional army of trained soldiers. The pharaoh was in charge of this army, and led his soldiers into battle. Egyptian soldiers used a variety of weapons including spears, daggers, axes, and bows and arrows.

Horse-drawn chariots
Specially trained soldiers fired arrows from horse-drawn chariots. Each chariot carried two soldiers and was pulled by horses.

Battle at sea

Ancient Egyptians used warships for battles at sea. During the reign of Ramses III, the Sea People attacked Egypt. Ramses sent a fleet of warships to defeat them.

Decorated prow

Steering oars

Oars for power when there was no wind

Alexander the Great conquered Egypt and made himself pharaoh.

The bow and arrow was the most important weapon used in warfare.

Shields and spears

Foot soldiers carried a strong shield and a long, deadly spear.

FUN FACT!

Soldiers who fought bravely in battle were awarded golden medals that looked like flies – for 'stinging' the enemy so successfully!

297

Buying and selling

Egyptian traders did not use money to buy and sell goods. They exchanged goods with foreign traders. This was called bartering. Egyptian merchants offered things such as cattle, gold and papyrus. In return they were given silver, cedar wood and ivory.

Market places
An ancient Egyptian town had its own market place, where people went to buy food, pots, pans and other everyday goods.

Market stalls sold all kinds of fruits and vegetables

Egyptians took their goods to market to exchange for other items

Trading by sea
Ancient Egyptians traded with other countries along the river Nile. They reached them by boat.

Merchants brought exotic goods such as **elephant tusks** into Egypt.

Egyptians traded with other countries for **gems**, wood, oil and horses.

Goods were weighed to see how much they were worth

FUN FACT!

Fly swatters made from giraffe tails were a popular fashion item in ancient Egypt.

299

Farming the land

The farming year was divided into three seasons – the flood, the growing period and the harvest. After the floods, farmers prepared the soil and planted the seeds by hand. Then came the harvest, when the crops were gathered.

Fertile land
The river Nile used to flood its banks in July each year. The flood waters left a strip of rich black soil along each bank. The rest of the land was mainly just sand.

Gathering the grain
Workers gathered the grain by throwing the grain and chaff (grain shell) into the air. The heavier grain dropped to the floor.

Owning cattle

Tax collectors would often decide
how rich people were by counting
how many cattle they owned.
Farmers had to pay the tax with
part of their harvest.

FUN FACT!

Sometimes farmers hired
flute players to keep
people company while
they worked.

Fruits and vegetables
grew well in the strips of
rich, dark soil.

A **shaduf** was used for
lifting water from the
Nile.

Quiz time!

1 Who was in charge of the underworld?

2 What did the Egyptians use as
fly swatters?

3 Who was in charge
of the army?

Q1 Picture clue

Answers 1 Osiris and Isis 2 Giraffe tails 3 The pharaoh

The working life

Most people worked as craftworkers or farm labourers, including potters, carpenters, weavers, jewellers and shoemakers. Scribes were important people because they knew how to read and write. They kept records of daily events.

Working for the pharaoh
Craftworkers had special areas within the town where they produced statues and furniture for the pharaoh.

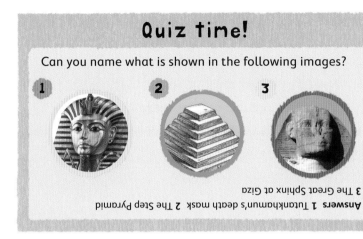
Workers often made a living by selling their goods at the market.

A **typical lunch** for a worker was bread and onions, washed down with beer.

Becoming a scribe
Only the sons of scribes went to school to learn how to read and write. Then they could be scribes, too.

Rich families had **servants**, who worked as maids, cooks and gardeners.

Life at home

Egyptian houses were made from mud bricks. The inside walls were covered with thick plaster, which helped keep the houses cool in the hot weather. Wealthy Egyptians lived in countryside villas. Poorer families lived in a crowded single room.

Family life

The centre of Egyptian life was family and many different generations of people shared a home together. The man was always the head of the household.

Children played with wooden or clay toys

Quiz time!

1 What did Egyptians decorate tombs with?

2 Which part of the body was left inside a mummy?

3 What is the name of the device used for lifting water?

4 Who knew how to read and write?

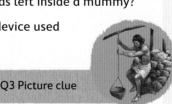

Q3 Picture clue

Answers 1 Paintings **2** The heart **3** Shaduf **4** Scribes

Mud was shaped into bricks and left to dry in the Sun.

Senet was a popular board game

Oil lamps made of clay were used as lights.

The dwarf god, Bes, was the god of the home.

The Egyptians used woven papyrus mats instead of carpets

305

Dressing up

Both men and women wore make-up. The Egyptians believed that a black eye paint, called kohl, had magical healing powers and could cure poor eyesight and fight eye infections.

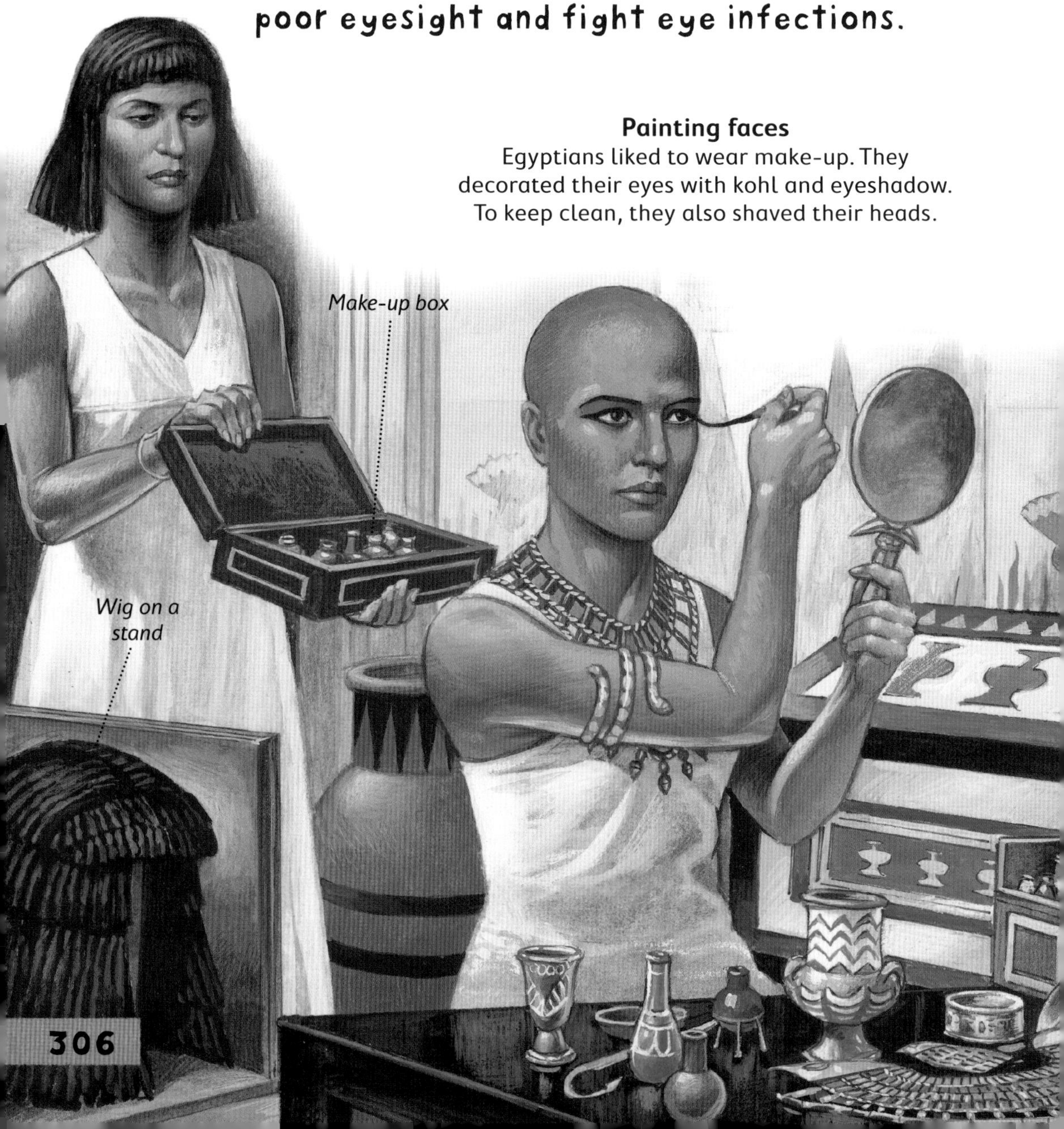

Painting faces
Egyptians liked to wear make-up. They decorated their eyes with kohl and eyeshadow. To keep clean, they also shaved their heads.

Make-up box

Wig on a stand

306

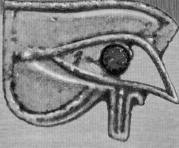

The eye of Horus was a good luck charm worn by Egyptians.

Wearing wigs
Wealthy people wore wigs made from human hair or sheep's wool. They were stored on stands in the home.

Hair care
Egyptians looked after their hair and wigs with combs made of wood and ivory.

Clothes were made from linen to keep people cool in hot weather.

Make a magic eye charm

You will need
clay • paints • paintbrush • varnish

1 Shape the clay into the eye of Horus, shown here.

2 Leave the clay to harden.

3 Paint your charm with bright colours and leave it to dry. Varnish it to make it look extra shiny!

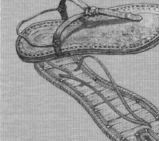

Sandals were made from papyrus and other reeds (bottom). Rich people wore leather ones (top).

Travelling by boat

The main method of transport was by boat along the river Nile. The Nile is the world's longest river, flowing across the entire length of Egypt. Early boats were made from papyrus reeds.

Transporting mummies
The mummified body of an Egyptian pharaoh was transported by boat across the river Nile. It would then be buried in its pyramid tomb.

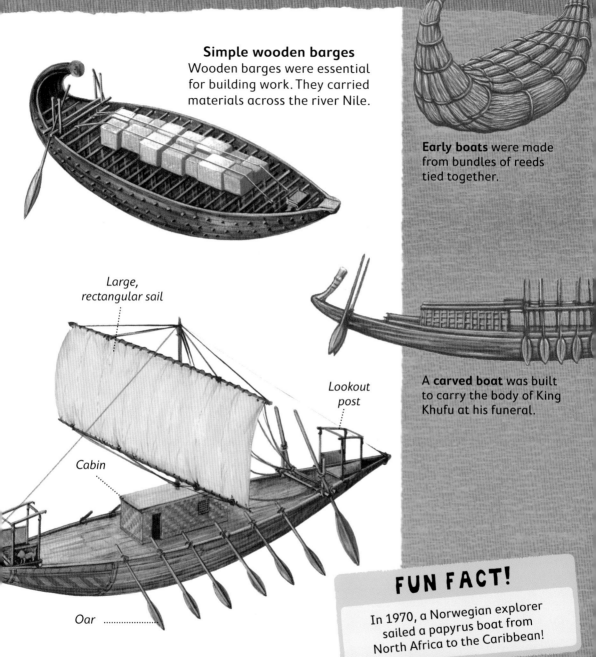

Simple wooden barges
Wooden barges were essential for building work. They carried materials across the river Nile.

Early boats were made from bundles of reeds tied together.

A **carved boat** was built to carry the body of King Khufu at his funeral.

Large, rectangular sail

Lookout post

Cabin

Oar

FUN FACT!
In 1970, a Norwegian explorer sailed a papyrus boat from North Africa to the Caribbean!

Wooden-built trading ships
Trading ships used both sail and oar power. They were kept close to the shore, and fitted with a large rectangular sail and a few oars.

Painting words

The ancient Egyptians used a system of picture-writing called hieroglyphics. Each hieroglyph, or picture, represented an object or sound. The insides of tombs were decorated with hieroglyphs, often showing scenes from the dead person's life.

Painting tombs

Several artists worked together to paint tombs with colourful symbols and scenes. The Egyptians believed the scenes would come to life in the next world.

A senior artist checked and corrected the outlines, then painted over them in black paint

A junior artist drew the outlines of the scenes

310

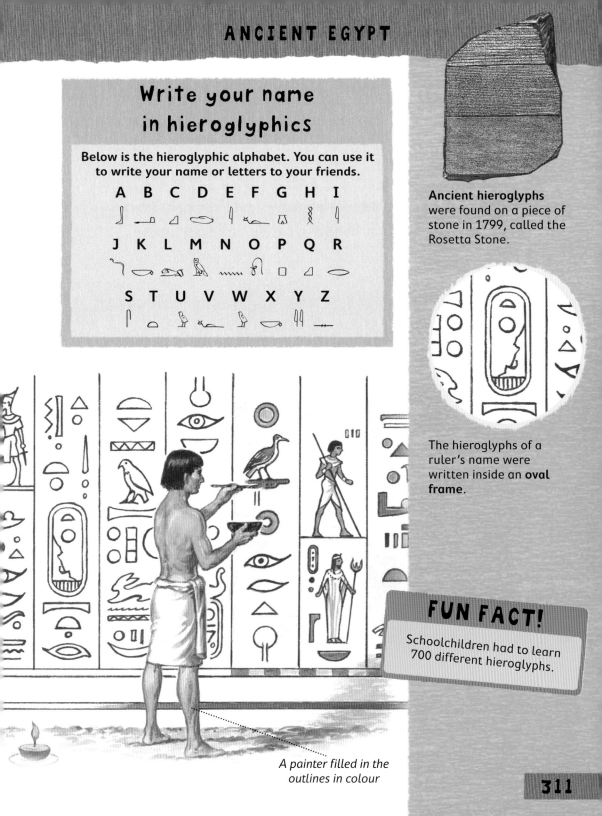

Write your name in hieroglyphics

Below is the hieroglyphic alphabet. You can use it to write your name or letters to your friends.

A B C D E F G H I

J K L M N O P Q R

S T U V W X Y Z

Ancient hieroglyphs were found on a piece of stone in 1799, called the Rosetta Stone.

The hieroglyphs of a ruler's name were written inside an **oval frame**.

FUN FACT!

Schoolchildren had to learn 700 different hieroglyphs.

A painter filled in the outlines in colour

311

Egyptian know-how

The Egyptians were the first to write on a
kind of paper made from papyrus reeds.
They also used their knowledge of the stars
to help build temples. Doctors understood
the basic workings of the human body.

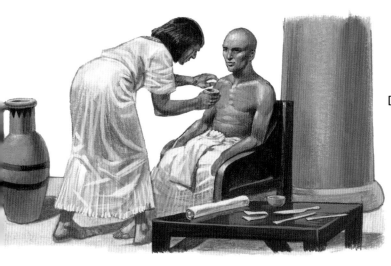

Egyptian medicine
Doctors knew how to set
broken bones and treat
illnesses such as fevers.

Taking measurements
The Egyptians used a device
called a nilometer to measure
the depth of the river Nile.
They put measuring posts in
the riverbed to check the
water levels.

Making a papyrus sheet

Papyrus was expensive because it took such a long time to make.

Papyrus scrolls were the first kind of paper ever used.

Firstly, the papyrus stems were chopped down and cut into lots of thin strips.

Then the strips were laid in rows on a frame to form layers.

Ink was made by mixing water with charcoal or coloured minerals.

The strips were then pressed under weights. This squeezed out the water and squashed the layers together.

Finally, when the papyrus was dry, the surface was rubbed with a stone to make it smooth for writing.

Reed brushes were used for writing on papyrus.

313

ANCIENT ROME

The Roman Empire

An empire is made up of many different countries ruled by one person — the emperor. Rome in Italy was once the centre of a great empire. It became rich and powerful, ruling more than 50 million people around the world.

Key

1 Slaves captured during battle were tied up and walked through the city.

2 Soldiers marched through Rome to celebrate a victory at war.

3 The emperor led the victory parade on a golden chariot.

1

Capital city
More than one million people lived in Rome and by AD 300, it was the largest city in the world.

Hustle and bustle

The city of Rome was busy, noisy and exciting, with many beautiful buildings.

Romans bought goods from **stalls** in the market square.

Temples were built so people could worship the gods.

2

3

FUN FACT!

The largest sewer in ancient Rome was so high and wide that a horse and cart could drive through it!

Building Rome

The Romans invented new building materials, such as concrete. They also discovered how to build arches, and invented pumps to push water uphill.

Amphitheatres were used for performances

Time to shop

The Romans built the first ever 'shopping mall'. It was called Trajan's Market. There were 150 shops on five levels, as well as a large main hall.

Brilliant builders

The Romans were amazing builders and architects. Their roads and many of their buildings have lasted more than 2000 years.

Each day, **aqueducts** brought fresh water from the hills into Rome.

Water from aqueducts came out of **fountains**.

Domes were designed for the roofs of large buildings

Arches were built in honour of the emperor

319

Rulers of Rome

For a long time, Rome was ruled by kings. It beame a republic – a state without a king – after many years of fighting. An army general called Octavian took power and became the first emperor, bringing peace to Rome.

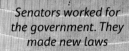

Senators worked for the government. They made new laws

Julius Caesar
In 47 BC, a successful general called Julius Caesar declared himself dictator. His reign ended in 44 BC when he was killed.

Roman law

Everyone in Rome had to obey the laws, which were very strict. If someone was accused of a serious crime, they attended court to see if they were innocent or guilty.

Roman coins showed the most powerful people of the time, usually the emperor.

Octavian became the first Roman emperor in 27 BC. He introduced many laws.

The public could watch the court from galleries

A lawyer, called an advocatus, helped the accused person

A person accused of a crime had to go to court

FUN FACT!

The mad Emperor Nero was said to have laughed and played music while watching a terrible fire destroy part of Rome.

Gods and goddesses

The Romans worshipped many gods and goddesses. The emperor offered sacrifices to the gods who protected Rome. Ordinary Romans made offerings of food, wine and incense.

Gods everywhere
There was a god for almost everything, from love and war to wild animals and people's homes.

Jupiter, king of the gods

Mars, god of war

Juno, queen of the gods

Neptune, god of the sea

Venus, goddess of love

322

Roman and Greek names

The Romans and Greeks worshipped the same gods, but used different names for them.

ROMAN	GREEK
Jupiter	Zeus
Mars	Ares
Venus	Aphrodite
Neptune	Poseidon
Minerva	Athena
Diana	Artemis

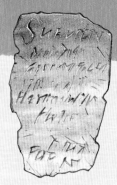

People wrote **messages** to the gods asking them to curse their enemies.

A family **shrine** was like a mini church inside people's homes.

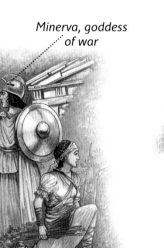

Minerva, goddess of war

Mercury, messenger of the gods

Diana, goddess of the moon and hunting

Pan, god of the mountainside, pastures, sheep and goats

FUN FACT!

After an animal had been sacrificed to the gods, a priest examined its liver. If it was diseased, bad luck was on the way!

The people of Rome

By around AD 300, Rome was the
largest city in the world. The
government was run by rich nobles
and knights. Ordinary citizens
were poor, but they could vote
and serve in the army. Slaves
had no rights at all.

The Forum
At the heart of the city was a
large marketplace called the
Forum. It was surrounded by
government buildings.

Slave trade

Slaves were bought and sold at slave-markets. They were shown to the citizens to be chosen or rejected. Sometimes they were set free by their owners.

City guards protected Rome from outside attackers.

Senators were important government leaders.

Meeting place

People went to the Forum to meet their friends and people they worked with, to listen to famous speakers, or to talk with others about important matters.

FUN FACT!

Roman engineers also designed public lavatories. These lavatories were not private. Users sat on rows of seats, side by side!

325

Family life

A Roman family included servants as well as a husband, wife and their children. In rich families, the servants had their own quarters within the villas (homes).

Herbs were ground to put in sauces

Cooking together
Families spent much of their time in the kitchen. Servants helped the women of the household to prepare the meals.

Wine and oil were stored in large pots

Lying down

At banquets, Romans ate lying down on couches around a main table. They took off their sandals before entering the dining room.

Banquet food included roast meats, wine and dates.

Charcoal was burned in the stove

Ordinary people could buy **ready-cooked snacks** from roadside stalls.

Olives could be pickled and eaten with bread, or crushed to make oil.

At home

Wealthy Romans lived in large houses in the country called villas. These houses were normally surrounded by orchards, fields of wheat and flocks of sheep.

Beautiful homes
The first villas were simple farmhouses. As Rome became richer, villas became magnificent mansions.

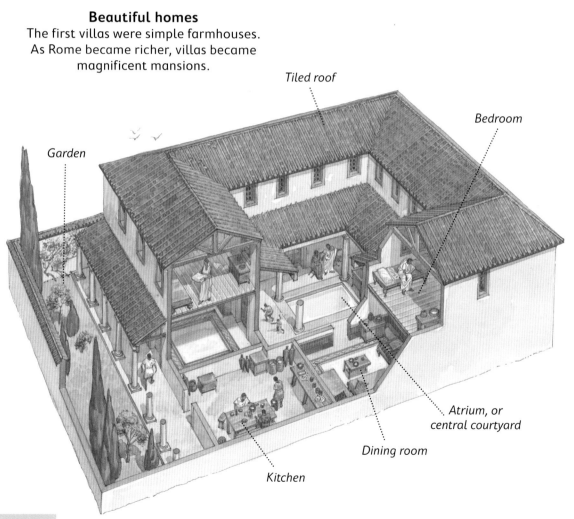

Tiled roof

Bedroom

Garden

Atrium, or central courtyard

Dining room

Kitchen

Keeping warm

Wealthy families had underfloor central heating in their homes. The heat came from a fire burning beneath the floor.

Space in the walls for hot air to move around

Rome's **fire fighters** were specially trained slaves.

A fire to create heat

Space under the floor for hot air to move around

Villas often had **pools** in their courtyards. They were only for decoration.

Make a mosaic

You will need

pencil • paper • glue • squares cut from coloured paper

1 Draw the outline of your design – perhaps a fish – on a large sheet of paper.

2 Stick the coloured squares onto the large sheet of paper, following the outlines of your design to create a Roman mosaic.

In cities, many Romans lived in **blocks of flats** called 'insulae'.

A trip to the baths

Roman baths were places to wash, relax, meet friends and get fit. Visitors could have a massage or a haircut. They could also buy scented oils and perfumes, read a book, eat, or admire works of art.

The frigidarium had the coldest pool

Luxury baths

One of the most popular baths was at Aquae Sulis (Bath). It had changing rooms and lockers, as well as hot, warm and cold baths.

Fires heated the water for the hot rooms

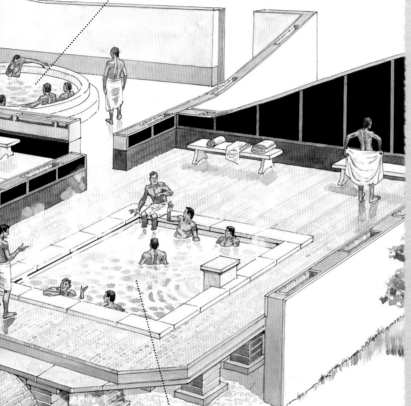

The tepidarium had a cool or lukewarm pool

The hot room was called the caldarium

Bathtime

Men and women were not allowed to bathe together. Women usually went to the baths in the mornings, while the men were at work. Men then went in the afternoons.

A **massage** was the perfect way to relax.

Baths were a good place to **meet friends** for a chat.

Washing was done without soap. Romans scraped dirt off instead!

331

Roman style

What a Roman wore depended on how important they were. Ordinary men and women wore plain white togas made of rough material. Rich people wore robes made of fine-quality wool and silk.

Everyday clothes
At the height of the empire, women wore brightly coloured robes and shawls. Children wore knee-length tunics.

A laurel wreath signified an honour from the government

Brightly coloured silk from China showed wealth

Purple was the most expensive dye in ancient Rome

Wear a Roman toga

1 Drape a white sheet over your left shoulder. Then pass the rest behind your back.

2 Pull the sheet across your front, so that you're wrapped up in it.

3 Finally, drape the last end over your right hand and there you have it, a Roman toga!

A Roman **comb** was made of ivory, bone or wood.

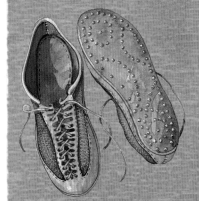

Roman **shoes** had studs to stop them wearing down too quickly.

Gems and jewels

Roman women wore fine jewellery made of gold and pearls. A shiny black stone called jet was carved into bangles and beads.

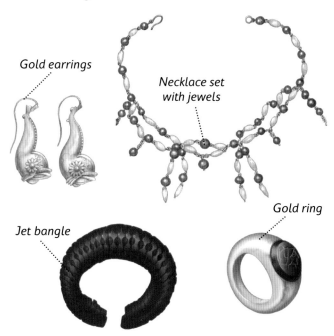

Gold earrings

Necklace set with jewels

Jet bangle

Gold ring

Hairstyles took a long time to fix and were kept in place with pins.

School days

Roman boys learnt three main subjects –
reading, maths and public speaking. They
went to school from 7 to 16 years old.
Most girls did not go to school.

Time to learn
Roman schoolboys were often
taught by Greek schoolmasters.
Learning to read and write were
some of the most important skills.

Numerals

I	1	VI	6
II	2	VII	7
III	3	VI	8
IV	4	IX	9
V	5	X	10

Easy reading
Romans often read
standing up as it was an
easier way to read a
papyrus scroll.

1,2,3...
Children used a counting frame called an abacus to help them to count.

Wax tablets were used to write on.

Learning skills
Girls from rich families were taught to cook, clean and play instruments, such as the lyre.

A **stylus** (right) was used to write on a wax tablet. Pens (left) were used to write on papyrus.

Let's speak Latin

puer	*POO-er*	boy
puella	*poo-ELL-a*	girl
miles	*MEE-lays*	soldier
mare	*MAH-ray*	sea
insula	*IN-soo-lah*	island
equus	*ec-WUSS*	horse

Ink was made of soot, vinegar and sticky gum. It was stored in a pot.

Work and play

The Romans liked music and dancing. They played instruments such as pipes, cymbals and horns. In their free time, many Romans enjoyed going to the theatre.

Entertainment
Musicians and dancers were popular entertainment at parties and banquets. They played instruments such as tambourines, cymbals and wooden pipes.

FUN FACT!

Roman actors were so popular that women couldn't sit near the stage in case they tried to arrange a date with one of the stars!

Theatre fun

Romans enjoyed acting in plays, but only men were allowed on stage. For women's roles, men wore masks and dressed in female costume.

Masks were often worn by actors to help identify the characters.

Street music

Buskers played musical instruments in the streets, and they could even be hired for parties.

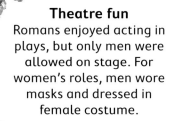

Women made their own clothes by **spinning wool** by hand.

The mighty Colosseum

The Colosseum was a huge oval arena in the centre of Rome, which could seat 50,000 people. It was built of stone, concrete and marble and had 80 separate entrances. It was used for gladiator fights and pretend sea battles.

Gladiator battles

Gladiators had to fight in the arena until they died. A wounded fighter pleads for his life by showing a thumbs-up sign. If the crowd thought he should die, the people showed a thumbs-down sign.

6

5

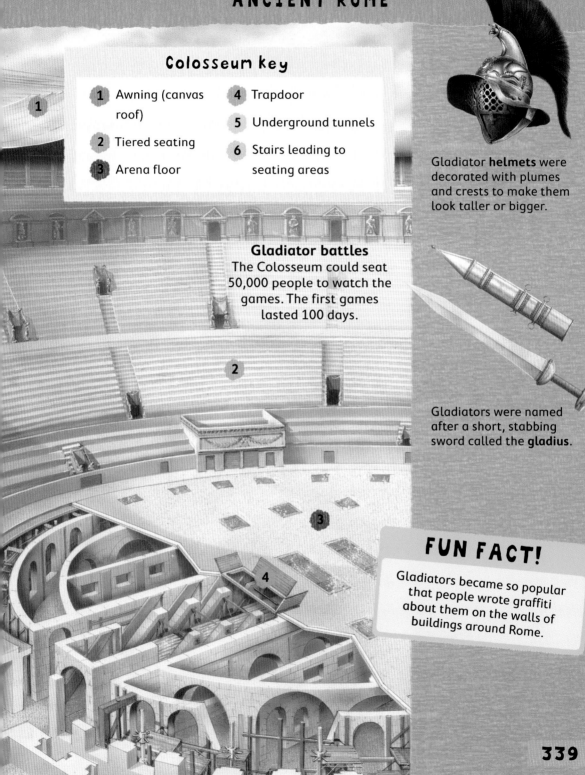

Colosseum key

1 Awning (canvas roof)

2 Tiered seating

3 Arena floor

4 Trapdoor

5 Underground tunnels

6 Stairs leading to seating areas

Gladiator **helmets** were decorated with plumes and crests to make them look taller or bigger.

Gladiator battles
The Colosseum could seat 50,000 people to watch the games. The first games lasted 100 days.

Gladiators were named after a short, stabbing sword called the **gladius**.

FUN FACT!

Gladiators became so popular that people wrote graffiti about them on the walls of buildings around Rome.

In the army

The Roman Empire needed troops to defend its land against enemy attack. It was a dangerous job, but the soldiers were well paid and cared for. After around 25 years of service, they were given money or land.

Tortoise shell

During battles, soldiers used their shields to make a protective 'shell' called a testudo, or tortoise. Their shields were placed at all sides.

Quiz time!

1 Where did the Romans go to get clean?

2 What did ordinary men and women wear?

3 At what age did boys go to school?

4 What did children use to help them count?

Q4 Picture clue

Answers 1 Baths 2 Togas 3 7 to 16 years old 4 Abacus

Roman cavalry soldiers rode horses and helped the foot soldiers during battle.

On the move

The Roman army marched around the empire to where they were needed. They travelled up to 30 kilometres a day!

Roman armour was made from metal strips held together by straps and buckles.

FUN FACT!

Roman soldiers kept warm in cold countries by wearing woolly underpants beneath their tunics!

Roman roads

Rome's first main road was built in 312 BC. The city was at the centre of a huge road network that stretched for more than 85,000 kilometres. This system made it easier for the Roman army and leaders to travel around the empire.

Speedy service
The most important travellers on the roads were official messengers who rode on horseback.

Drainage ditches were added to take away water when it rained

The route was accurately marked out before building

Straight through

To make travel as quick as possible, roads were built in straight lines, taking the shortest route.

A road engineer used a tool called a **groma** to measure straight lines.

Stone slabs were slotted together for a smooth road surface

Stone pillars were put up to show distances between towns.

FUN FACT!

The Romans would often consult a priest or fortune-teller before setting out on a long journey.

The road was made of layers of earth and stones, on top of a solid foundation

KNIGHTS AND CASTLES

Life in the Middle Ages

In the Middle Ages, between 470 and 1450, many castles and forts were built. A castle provided shelter for a king or lord and his family, and helped him to defend his lands.

346

The **drawbridge** was the entrance to the castle.

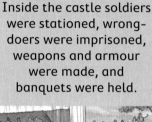

Important place
Inside the castle soldiers were stationed, wrong-doers were imprisoned, weapons and armour were made, and banquets were held.

Banquets (feasts) were held in the **Great Hall**.

Key

1. Soldiers practised their fighting skills in the castle grounds
2. Peasants farmed the land around the castle
3. Animals were kept for food and transport
4. The castle had strong walls and defences
5. Knights were soldiers who fought on horseback

The lord and his family had a private living area called the **solar**.

The first castles

The first castles were mostly built from wood. They were not very strong and caught fire easily, so from around 1100 onwards, castles were built in stone. A stone castle gave better protection against attack, fire and bad weather.

Protective walls
A stone castle often had two walls, an outer and an inner wall, to give extra protection from attackers.

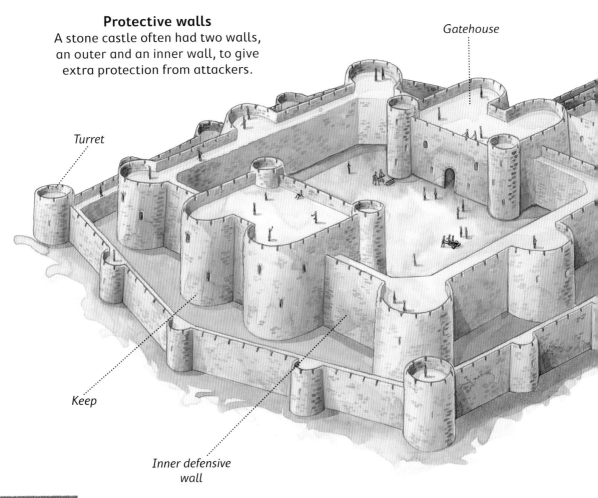

Gatehouse

Turret

Keep

Inner defensive wall

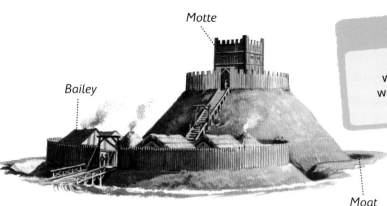

Motte

Bailey

Moat

FUN FACT!

The builders of the early wooden castles covered the walls with wet leather to stop them from burning down.

Deep ditch

Castle builders dug a deep ditch, called a moat, around the outside of the motte and bailey castle. This was to stop attackers reaching the castle walls.

Outer defensive wall

Japanese castles were built with different layers.

Design a castle

You will need:
pencil • paper • colouring pens

1 Draw a plan of your ideal castle, making sure it has plenty of defences. Will it have arrow slits? Will the walls be high? Will it have a moat running around it?

2 Don't forget to design a drawbridge to let the lord and his family in and out of their castle.

The **fence** around the motte used pieces of pointed wood to make it harder for the enemy to climb over.

Building castles

The best place to build a castle was on top of a hill. A hilltop position gave good views over the surrounding countryside, making it harder for an enemy to launch a surprise attack.

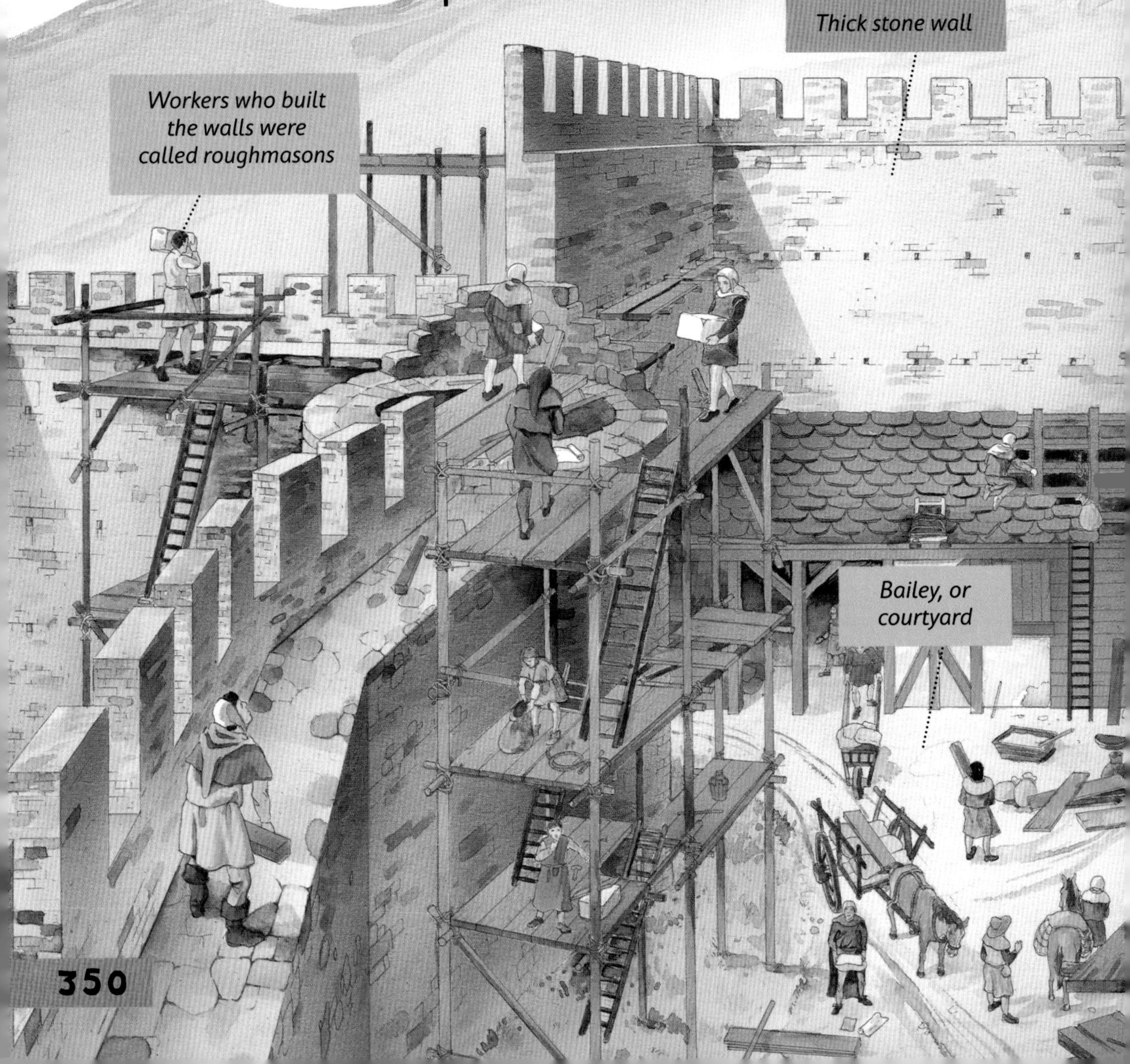

Thick stone wall

Workers who built the walls were called roughmasons

Bailey, or courtyard

The keep was the safest part of the castle, where the lord lived

Waterworks

Inside the castle was a courtyard called a bailey. A thick wall was built around it. Most castles got water from a well that was dug inside the bailey. A large water wheel was used to draw the water up.

The **keep** had banquet rooms and bedrooms for the lord and his family.

Water wheel

The master mason was in charge of the workers

Well

Heavy materials were placed in buckets and pulled up to where they were needed.

Workers carried stones, dug trenches and mixed mortar (sand and water).

Inside the castle

Stone castles were cold, damp places. Cold winds blew through the windows, which had no glass. There was no heating or running water.

House and home
The lord and lady did not live inside the castle alone. Servants and knights also had their own quarters. Even prisoners stayed in the castle – in the dungeon.

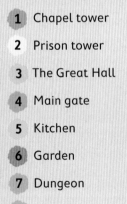

Key

1 Chapel tower

2 Prison tower

3 The Great Hall

4 Main gate

5 Kitchen

6 Garden

7 Dungeon

8 Bedroom

Kitchens were built far from the rest of the castle in case they caught fire.

Quiz time!

1 When were the Middle Ages?

2 What was the courtyard at the bottom of a castle called?

3 What were the first castles made of?

4 What is the name of the ditch that surrounds a castle?

Q2 Picture clue

Answers **1** Between 470 and 1450 **2** Bailey **3** Wood **4** Moat

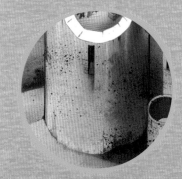

Dungeons were dark, slimy prisons.

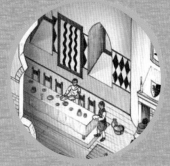

Tapestries on the castle walls helped to warm the rooms.

Who's who?

A castle was the home of an important and powerful person, such as a king, lord or knight. The lord controlled the castle itself, as well as the lands and people around it. The lady of the castle was in charge of the day-to-day running.

In charge
The master of the horse had to look after the lord's horses.

354

Metal makers

The castle blacksmith made iron shoes for all the horses. The armourer made weapons and armour for the army.

Armourer

Blacksmith

The steward was in charge of all the servants.

Servants cooked, cleaned and ran errands.

Protecting the people

Local villagers were allowed to shelter inside the castle walls when their lands were under attack.

FUN FACT!

The servants didn't have their own bathroom. They had to take a dip in the local river to wash — and to get rid of any fleas and lice!

People and power

In the Middle Ages, the king or queen was the most important person in the country. The king gave land to his barons and other noblemen. In return, they supplied the king with soldiers and weapons to fight wars.

Religion and ruler
In the Middle Ages, the Church and the ruler of the country were both very powerful, so they had to try to work together.

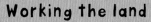

Working the land

In the Middle Ages, 90 percent of people worked on the land. Everything they had, including their animals, food and clothes, belonged to the lord.

KNIGHTS AND CASTLES

Barons were the most powerful noblemen.

Knights defended the king and lords from their enemies.

Quiz time!

1 Who was in charge of the castle?

2 Where was the best place to build a castle?

3 Who made shoes for the horses?

4 Which room was built far away from the other rooms in case it caught fire?

Q3 Picture clue

Answers **1** Lord and lady **2** On a hill **3** Blacksmith **4** Kitchen

Peasants were the poorest people of the land.

357

Knight school

The sons of noblemen were sent to a lord's house when they were seven years old. They spent 14 years with the lord, training to become knights. If they were good enough, they became knights at the age of 21.

Knights in training
At the age of seven, a boy was taught how to ride a horse and how to shoot a bow and arrow. He then became a squire, or assistant, where he learned how to fight with a sword.

Swords with two sharp edges were used by knights in the Middle Ages.

The dubbing ceremony
The ceremony of making a new knight was known as dubbing. A knight had to pray all night in church before his dubbing ceremony took place.

A mace had deadly spikes to pierce armour.

A new knight
During the dubbing ceremony, a lord or another knight tapped the new knight on the shoulder with a sword.

A **rich knight** had three horses for fighting, riding and carrying heavy loads.

359

Jousting tournaments

Knights often took part in pretend battles called tournaments. Tournaments were good practice for the real thing – war. Knights divided into two sides and fought each other as if in a proper battle.

Knights aimed to hit their opponent's head, chest or shield with their lance

Lances were made of metal. Their tips were not sharp, so knights didn't get seriously injured

Create your own shield

You will need
coloured pens • paper

1 Draw a big shield shape on a piece of paper.

2 On the shield, draw a symbol for your family – perhaps swords or a crown.

3 Colour in your shield, then hang it on your bedroom door to show everyone that you're a knight!

In competition

Jousting was a fight between two knights on horseback. Each knight tried to win by knocking the other off his horse.

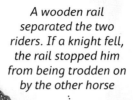

A wooden rail separated the two riders. If a knight fell, the rail stopped him from being trodden on by the other horse

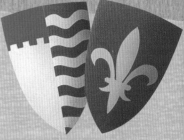

Coats of arms were badges worn by knights so others could recognize them.

Banners displayed a knight's own personal design.

FUN FACT!

Some knights cheated in jousts by wearing special armour that was fixed onto the horse's saddle!

Dress for battle

Early knights wore a type of armour called chainmail. It was made of thousands of tiny iron rings joined to each other. Gradually, knights began to wear more and more armour. By the 1400s, they were wearing full suits of steel armour.

Caring for armour
Armour was stored in a room called the armoury. It was melted and cleaned by the armourer and his workmen. It could take an hour to dress a knight for battle.

Shields and tunics were decorated with a knight's coat of arms

Gauntlets were gloves made of leather. They had steel plates stitched to the outside

Knights were dressed by squires (assistants). The armour was put on from the feet upwards

Armour made of metal plates gave the best protection

A **wool tunic** was worn over the top of a knight's armour.

Chainmail was a kind of 'knitted' metal armour.

FUN FACT!

French knights wore shoes with pointed toes. When they needed to make a quick escape in battle, they had to cut the points off to run away!

363

Into battle

Battles were fough to end disagreements or to gain land, wealth and power. Knights and soldiers fought for the lord. In return, the lord looked after them or gave them land.

Building defences
Knights marched or rode into battle carrying the flag and coat of arms of their lord. Ordinary soldiers fought on foot.

Quiz time!

1 How long is the Bayeux Tapestry?

2 What were the followers of King Arthur called?

3 Who killed a fierce dragon in the famous legend?

Q2 Picture clue

Answers **1** 70 metres **2** Knights of the Round Table **3** St George

Knights with **armoured horses** were put on the front row during battle.

Weapons at the ready
Knights had two main weapons — the sword and the shield. They also fought with lances (long wooden spears), daggers and axes.

Knights used a weapon called the morning star — a spiked ball on the end of a chain.

FUN FACT!

Soldiers called 'retrievers' had to run into the middle of the battle and collect all the spare arrows!

Brave knights

Many famous stories, or legends, have been written about knights and their bravery. The legend of St George tells how he killed a fierce dragon. King Arthur became king after pulling a magic sword, called Excalibur, out of a stone.

Fiery battle
St George killed the dragon that was eating the people of Lydia, in Turkey, when the people agreed to become Christians.

Love triangle

Lancelot was King Arthur's favourite knight. Lancelot fell in love with Arthur's wife, Guinevere. This caused great upset in the court.

El Cid was a Spanish knight who fought against the Moors of North Africa.

The Black Prince was a great English warrior.

Quiz time!

1 What was the ceremony of making a new knight called?

2 What type of armour did early knights wear?

3 What were a knight's two main weapons in battle?

4 How long did it take to train a knight?

Q3 Picture clue

Answers **1** Dubbing **2** Chainmail **3** Sword and shield **4** 14 years

King Arthur had followers called the Knights of the Round Table.

Famous battles

Between 1337 and 1453, England and France were at war. This was called the Hundred Years War. The two countries fought each other to decide who should control France. In the end the French won, and England lost all of its lands in France except for the port of Calais.

Young leader
In 1429, a young French girl called Joan of Arc led the French army against the English. After ten days, the English were defeated.

The Bayeux Tapestry

The Bayeux Tapestry is over 70 metres long. It records the story of the Norman invasion of England in 1066.

William the Conqueror claimed that he should be king of England.

Caltrops were star-shaped pieces of metal that were scattered on the ground to stop horses.

FUN FACT!

If a knight was captured alive during battle, he could be offered back to his family in return for a generous amount of money!

Castle siege

A siege is when an enemy surrounds a castle and stops all supplies from reaching the people inside. The idea is to starve them until they surrender or die.

The trebuchet fired stones using an arm with a sling

Attack!
An attacking enemy needed to break through the castle's defences to get inside the walls. Knights and soldiers used as many weapons as possible, including giant catapults.

Knights surrounded the castle, waiting for the enemy to surrender

This gigantic catalpult fired large rocks at the walls

Attackers climbed ladders to try to get into the castle quickly

Inside a tower called a belfry, attackers could reach the top of the wall safely

FUN FACT!

The ropes used to wind up trebuchet machines were made from plaits of human hair!

Attackers dug **tunnels** under walls and towers. They then lit fires to make the towers collapse.

The battering ram was a heavy log used to attack gates and walls

Attackers were protected from arrows inside the **battering ram**.

Fighting back

An attacking enemy had to break through a castle's defences to get inside its walls. Defenders would pull up the castle drawbridge and lower an iron gate, called a portcullis.

Keeping them out

Defenders of the castle used many different methods to try to keep out their enemies. They threw stone missiles, fired arrows and even poured boiling water over the castle walls.

Key

1. Battlements along the top of the walls gave soldiers something to hide behind

2. The thick stone wall was difficult for attackers to break down

3. Heavy stones were thrown onto the enemy below

4. Archers fired arrows at the attackers

5. Boiling water was poured onto the heads of enemies

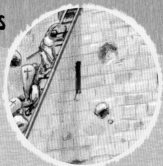

Archers would fire arrows at the enemy through **narrow slits** in the castle walls.

A **crossbow** was a more accurate weapon than a bow and arrow.

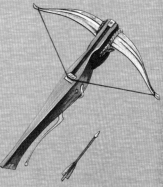

Archers stood on the castle walls and fired down at enemies.

INDEX

INDEX

ACKNOWLEDGEMENTS

The publishers would like to thank the following sources for the use of their photographs:

Key t=top, b=bottom, l=left, r=right, c=centre

COVER FRONT (jellyfish, tl) Vlad61, (train, tl) Tatiana Makotra, (ladybird, cl) irin-k, (toucan, r) Eduardo Rivero, (arch, bc) Mike Norton; BACK (F1 car, tc) David Acosta Allely

Dreamstime 69(tr) Phakimata; 114 Silverstore; 124 Paha_l

Fotolia 36–37(bg) Noel Powell; 67(tl) .shock, (tr) John Saxenian, (br) Melissa Schalke; 72(bl); 73(tr) Urbanhearts; 79(br) Alexander Zotov; 111(l) Tomasz Trojanowski; 123(br) 2happy; 125(bl) photlook; 135(br) Jgz; 138–139 DX; 167(tr) AlienCat; 179(tl) zebra0209; 187(bl) Gail Johnson; 193(cr) rkwphotography; 195(t, third from left) filtv; 215(tr) Vibe Images; 241(cr) javarman; 275(tr) Henryk Dybka; 281(tr) WONG SZE FEI

iStockphoto.com 15(cr), 42–43(b), 46–47(b) Jan Rysavy; 23(tr) Carmen Martínez Banús; 29(br) Steven Wynn; 71(cr) Sean Randall, (br) pkruger; 73(b, second from left) Klaas Lingbeek–van Kranen, (b, third from left) Gertjan Hooijer; 131(cr) Brady Willette, (br) Tao Song; 141(cr) Steffen Foerster; 169(tr) Joe McDaniel; 172(b) Michel de Nijs; 187(tl, picture c) Liz Leyden; 188–189 Richard Lindie; 249(cr) hilton kotze; 344–345 iñaki antoñana plaza

NASA 16 NASA Jet Propulsion Laboratory (NASA–JPL); 23(br) NASA Jet Propulsion Laboratory (NASA–JPL); 25(l), (br) NASA Jet Propulsion Laboratory (NASA–JPL); 31(bl) NASA Jet Propulsion Laboratory (NASA–JPL); 34–35 NASA Jet Propulsion Laboratory (NASA–JPL); 35(tl) NASA Marshall Space Flight Center (NASA–MSFC), (tr) NASA Jet Propulsion Laboratory (NASA–JPL), (br) NASA Jet Propulsion Laboratory (NASA–JPL); 39(br) NASA Jet Propulsion Laboratory (NASA–JPL); 40–41; 41(bl); 43(br) Dominic Cantin; 45(tl) NASA Jet Propulsion Laboratory (NASA–JPL), (cl) NASA Jet Propulsion Laboratory (NASA–JPL), (bl) NASA Marshall Space Flight Center (NASA–MSFC), (tr) NASA Jet Propulsion Laboratory (NASA–JPL), (br) NASA Johnson Space Center (NASA–JSC); 48(br) NASA Headquarters – Greatest Images of NASA (NASA–HQ–GRIN); 49(l, third from top) NASA Johnson Space Center (NASA–JSC); 53(tr) NASA Headquarters – Greatest Images of NASA (NASA–HQ–GRIN); 109(br)

Shutterstock.com 12–13 1971yes; 47(br) Pincasso; 50–51 Vulkanette; 55(bl) Muellek Josef, (cr) beboy; 59(tr) Tyler Boyes, (cr) Michal Baranski, (br) Tyler Boyes; 63(tl) Alexandr Zyryanov, (tr) Andrey_Popov, (br) Jakub Cejpek; 65(tl) Christian Vinces, (tr) Nataliya Hora, (br) arindambanerjee; 66(bl) Mogens Trolle; 67(cl) Qba from Poland, (bl) Qba from Poland; 68(cl) VLADJ55; 69(br) al coroza; 70–71 ricardomiguel.pt; 70(cl) Armin Rose; 71(tr) Kaido Karner; 72–73 Antonio Jorge Nunes; 73(tl) Eduardo Rivero, (bl) Janos Nameth, (cr) USBFCO, (br) Rena Schild; 74(bl) Ilja Mašík, (tr) Valery Bareta; 75(l) Nasser Buhamad, (cr) Christopher Meder – Photography, (br) Volodymyr Goinyk; 76(bl) dirkr; 78(l) Michael Klenetsky; 79(tr) mountainpix, (cr) Lee Prince; 81(tr) Rich Carey, (cr) tororo reaction, (br) Rich Carey; 82–83 kavram; 84 Rechitan Sorin, (cr) MarcelClemens; 85(tr) Paul Fleet, (cr) Triff, (br) Ilja Mašík; 86(tl) apdesign, (cl) Asaf Eliason, (bl) szefei; 87(l, t–b) Oleg Znamenskiy, John De Bord, kkaplin, PHB.cz (Richard Semik), sima, Sergey Toronto; 87(tr) haveseen, (cr) Asaf Eliason, (br) Brian Lasenby; 89(tr) Vishnevskiy Vasily, (cr) Fanfo, (br) iamluckylee; 90(b) artjazz, (t) Mark Bridger; 91(bl) S.Borisov, (tl) Michael Macsuga, (tr) jan kranendonk, (br) Ilja Mašík; 92 Kushch Dmitry; 93(tl) Thor Jorgen Udvang, (tr) Oleg_Mit, (br) Jhaz Photography; 94–95 Pichugin Dmitry; 94(bl) Jhaz Photography; 95(bl) Styve Reineck, (tr) Galyna Andrushko, (cr) Andrejs Jegorovs, (br) Loskutnikov; 96(tl) Mirec; 97(tr) Serg64, (cr) elen_studio, (br) Sergey Sergeev; 99(tl) Andy Z., (tr) Brian Nolan, (br) B747; 100 kornilov007; 101(bl) Sam DCruz, (bc) Tramper, (tr) pasphotography, (br) LivingCanvas; 102–103 Todd Shoemake; 103(tr) DarkOne, (br) javarman; 104 PhotoHouse; 105(tl) James Thew, (tr) pzAxe, (br) Gail Johnson; 106–107 bedecs; 108–109 jabiru; 109(tl) Songquan Deng,

ACKNOWLEDGEMENTS

(tr) Barnaby Chambers, (cr) Pablo Scapinachis; 110–111 Sergey Lavrentev; 112–113 Vakhrushev Pavel; 116(cr) Dmitriy Shironosov, (br) Jennifer Griner; 117(tr) Péter Gudella, (br) SergiyN; 118 vadim kozlovsky; 119(br) Olaru Radian–Alexandru; 120(b) Ray Hub; 121(tr) Smileus, (cr) dslaven, (br) Kodda; 122(bl) Sebastian Crocker; 123(l) Hywit Dimyadi; 125(tr) Eimantas Buzas, (cr) Emilia Stasiak, (br) asharkyu; 126 ifong; 127(tl) Viktor Gmyria, (tr) Zhukov Oleg, (cr) Benko Zsolt, (br) ayazad; 128(t) Evgeny Karandaev; 129(tl, all) Annette Shaff, (tr) Annette Shaff, (cr) Doodle Monster, (br) PaulPaladin; 130 Jaggat; 131(tl) michael rubin, (bl) Mike Flippo, (tr) rezachka; 135(tl) wim claes, (bl) indiangypsy; 136 beerkoff; 137(tr) Nikola Spasenoski, (cr) Vladimir Sazonov, (br) Alexander Raths; 165(br) Mana Photo; 170–171 Specta; 173(tr) Armin Rose, (br) neelsky; 174 Willyam Bradberry; 175(cl) Thomas Barrat (polar bear), ANP (frog), Mike Price (whale), ericlefrancais (walrus), (tr) Mogens Trolle, (cr) Rich Carey, (br) Abhindia; 178–179 Specta; 178(b) Eugene Sim; 180 Jim Agronick, (b) Undersea Discoveries; 181(tr) Krzysztof Odziomek, (cr) Ian Scott, (br) A Cotton Photo; 182(cr) David Thyberg; 183(br) ECOSTOCK; 184 IrinaK; 185(tl) nice pictures, (bl) Katherine Worzalla, (tr) VasikO; 186 M Rutherford; 187(tl) Arto Hakola (picture a), Alfie Photography (picture b), (tr) Charles Masters, (br) MindStorm; 189(br) Gentoo Multimedia Ltd.; 190–191 Johan Swanepoel; 193(br) pix2go; 195(tl) Meawpong3405, (t, second from left) creativex, (tr) Graeme Shannon, (cr) covenant, (br) EcoPrint; 197(tl) Donna Heatfield, (tr) Michael Sheehan, (br) Eric Gevaert; 199(l) Christian Musat, (tr) sunsetman, (cr) Christian Musat, (br) CreativeNature.nl; 201(tr) Alan Scheer, (cr) Sebastian Knight, (br) Rafael Ramirez Lee; 205(tl) Santia, (tr) Steve Bower, (br) EcoPrint; 206(t) Pefkos; 207(tr) Liquid Productions, LLC, (br) alanf; 208 Wild Arctic Pictures; 209(tr) Vladimir Melnik, (cr) samsem, (br) nialat; 211(bl) Marcelo Sanchez, (tr) jo Crebbin, (cr) Four Oaks, (br) Xavier MARCHANT; 213(tr) Ammit; 214 hainaultphoto; 215(tl) Hedrus, (cr) EcoPrint; 217(tl) Henk Paul, (bl) javarman, (tr) Kapu, (cr) Karel Gallas, (br) Robyn Butler; 218 Richard Seeley; 219(tr) Ron Hilton, (cr) JKlingebiel; 220–221 Charles Masters; 222 JinYoung Lee, (t) Steve Byland; 223(bl) Sue McDonald, (tr) Marcin Ciesielski/Sylwia Cisek, (cr) John Carnemolla, (br) David Evison, 224(tr) Eric Isselée, (b) Image Focus, 225(tl) Arto Hakola, (bl) Borislav Borisov, (tr) Johan Swanepoel, (br) Janelle Lugge, 226–227 BlueOrange Studio; 227(tl) Christian Wilkinson, (tr) Ammit, 229(tl) Ewan Chesser, (bl) Eric Isselée, (tr) Mary Beth Charles, (br) Gentoo Multimedia Ltd.; 230–231 Stargazer; 231(tl) Steve Byland, (bl) MartinMaritz, (tr) Robert Gregory, (br) GMH Photography; 232 Kane513; 233(tl) Johan Swanepoel, (tr) M.Camerin, (br) Florian Andronache; 234 MCarter; 235 Natalia Sinjushina & Evgeniy Meyke, (tr) Ariel Bravy, (cr) Steve Byland, (br) Stubblefield Photography; 236 Rich Lindie; 237(tl) Arto Hakola, (bl) Daniel Alvarez, (tr) Milan M Jurkovic, (br) Michael E. Miller; 240(tl) Mircea BEZERGHEANU; 241(tl) Karel Gallas, (bl) Joe Gough, (tr) Sari ONeal, (br) Villiers Steyn; 242(l) Mogens Trolle; 243(tr) Colin Edwards Photography, (cr) wim claes, (br) Justin Black; 244(l) dashingstock; 245(l),(tr) worldswildlifewonders, (cr) Eduardo Rivero, (br) Uryadnikov Sergey; 246 Gentoo Multimedia Ltd.; 247(l) Rob McKay, (tr) Jack Cronkhite, (cr) Francis Bossé, (br) Martin Fowler; 248(l) BogdanBoev, (r) Xander Fotografie; 249 Mogens Trolle, (tl) Borislav Borisov, (tr) Marcel Schauer, (br) pix2go; 250–251 Volodymyr; 252(t) dcb, (b) Tobik; 253(bl) Dusty Cline, (tr) Tomas Sereda, (br) Matthew Cole; 255(tl) irin–k, (tr) Karel Gallas, (cr) Kletr, (br) Volkov Alexey; 257(cr) epsylon_lyrae; 258 alslutsky; 259(tr) Jens Stolt, (cr) Alexey Stiop, (br) Smit; 260–261 alslutsky; 261(tl) kurt_G, (tr) Anton Balazh, (cr) Cosmin Manci, 265(cr) Sue Robinson; 268(t) vblinov, (b) Evgeniy Ayupov; 269(bl) mikeledray, (br) irin–k; 270(l) Johan Larson, (r) kurt_G; 271(bl) Anette Andersen, (tr) Wilm Ihlenfeld, (cr) olavs, (br) Tyler Fox; 272 Nick Stubbs; 273(tl) Dr. Morley Read; 275(tl) J Hindman, (br) D. Kucharski & K. Kucharska; 277(bl) Damian Herde; 279(tr) Henrik Larsson, (br) Cathy Keifer; 280(b) Vinicius Tupinamba; 281(bl) Pan Xunbin; 282–283 Dan Breckwoldt; 293(cr) Nestor Noci; 299(br) MarcelClemens; 314–315 WDG Photo

Every effort has been made to acknowledge the source and copyright holder of each picture. Miles Kelly Publishing apologises for any unintentional errors or omissions.